The
BIGGER
BOOK OF
GROSS
JOKES

The BIGGER BOOK OF GROSS JOKES

• • • • •

by Julius Alvin

Kensington Books

http://www.kensingtonbooks.com

KENSINGTON BOOKS are published by

Kensington Publishing Corp.
850 Third Avenue
New York, NY 10022

Kensington and the K logo Reg. U.S. Pat. & TM Off.

ISBN 1-57566-362-7

First Printing: December, 1998
10 9 8 7 6 5 4 3 2 1

Printed in the United States of America

"For this I sent you to college?"
—Julius Alvin's mother

"Does this mean the midnight buffet is canceled?"
—Passenger to Captain, on the *Titanic*,
April 14, 1912, 10:53 P.M.

"There's no one in my freezer except for some
Ben and Jerry!"
—Jeffrey Dahmer

CONTENTS

1
A
REALLY
GROSS
VARIETY

● ● ● ● ● ● ●

How do you know when a hospital patient has AIDS?

He gets his shots with a dart gun.

• • •

What's the difference between a wife and Jell-O?

Jell-O moves when you eat it.

• • •

How long do rednecks cook their meat?

Until the skid marks don't show.

• • •

Why do women have legs?

So you don't have to drag them into the bathroom to wash up after sex.

• • •

What's the true definition of child abuse?

A mother who dips her baby's thermometer in Bengay.

What's the difference between a congressman and happiness?

Money can't buy happiness.

• • •

What do women and condos have in common?

They both spend more time in your wallet than on your dick.

• • •

So the elderly couple died in a car accident and went straight to heaven. They were given a tour by St. Peter himself. St. Peter said, "Over here is your oceanside condominium. Right there are the tennis courts, and next to them is the golf course. The swimming pool is over there. If you need any refreshments, just push the first button you see."

When St. Peter left, the old man turned to his wife, "Shit, Helen, this is your fault."

"What do you mean?" the wife asked.

"If it wasn't for you and your lousy oat bran," the husband complained, "we could have been here five years ago!"

• • •

Why do bachelors like smart women?

Because opposites attract.

• • •

A Really Gross Variety

What's the best thing about masturbating?

You always have a good grip on yourself.

• • •

A ten-year-old kid asks his mother, "Is God black or white?"

His mother responds, "Son, God is both black and white."

The kid then asks, "Mom, is God a man or a woman?"

His mother replies, "God is both a man and a woman."

The kid now asks, "Mom, is God straight or gay?"

"God is both straight and gay," the mother says.

"Mom," the kid finally asks, "is God Michael Jackson?"

• • •

How can you spot the Jewish baby in a nursery?

He's the one with heartburn.

• • •

What do you give the man who has everything?

A woman to show him how to do it.

• • •

Why are parrots smarter than chickens?

There's no such thing as Kentucky Fried Parrot.

What's the last thing a tramp from New Jersey takes off?

Her bowling shoes.

• • •

How many men does it take to change a roll of toilet paper?

Who gives a shit?

• • •

Why did the gay pickpocket always come home empty-handed?

He was just browsing.

• • •

A man rushes into a saloon and starts knocking back shots of Jack Daniel's, as fast as the bartender can pour them.

"Trying to drown your sorrows?" the bartender asks.

"Yes, I am," the man admits.

"Take my advice, buddy, it doesn't work," the bartender tells him.

"You're telling me?" the man replies. "I can't get that damn kid to go anywhere near the water!"

• • •

A Really Gross Variety

So Ed goes to see a psychiatrist to complain about his oversexed girlfriend.

Ed says, "My Sheila will stop at nothing to satisfy her lustful, kinky desires and bottomless sexual cravings. What can I do?"

The shrink says, "Tell her to make an appointment with me immediately."

• • •

Hear about the Australian guys who came late to the gay Olympics?

They couldn't get out of Sydney.

• • •

What goes in stiff but comes out soft?

Wrigley's Spearmint.

• • •

Why did the JAP write her zip code on her belly?

So her lover would come faster.

• • •

What's the definition of a Tampax?

Clitty-litter.

• • •

Then there was the ninety-year-old man who married a twenty-year-old girl.

All his friends had it in for him.

So little Timmy the Boy Scout comes home with a hand grenade in his pants. His mother says to him, "What's that in your trousers?"

Timmy answers, "A hand grenade."

His mother inquires, "Why do you have a hand grenade in your pants?"

"The next time the scoutmaster tries to grab my cock, I'll blow his fucking fingers off," Timmy declares.

• • •

So the Polish housewife tried to surprise her husband on his birthday by putting on a pair of crotchless panties. When her mate came home, she was lying on the rug, spreading her legs. "You want some of this?" she asked.

"Shit no," the Polack said. "Look what it's done to your undies."

• • •

What was the lesbian's favorite ice cream flavor?

Sardine.

• • •

How do you know when your wife is really ugly?

The waiter puts her plate on the floor.

• • •

A Really Gross Variety

How do you know when your kid's really a sadist?

He gets a girl pregnant just so he can watch the rabbit die.

· · ·

Why are men like lawn mowers?

They're hard to get started, and they only work half the time.

· · ·

What's the definition of a true genius?

A nudist with a memory for faces.

· · ·

So Murray goes to see his physician, who gives him an X ray, blood tests, and an EKG, followed by another half dozen tests.

"Murray," the doctor begins, "I've got good news and I've got bad news."

"What's the good news?" Murray wants to know.

"The good news is, my son just got accepted to Harvard law school."

"And what's the bad news?" Murray asks.

"You're going to pay for it."

· · ·

Why did the Polack throw away his toilet brush?

It hurt his asshole too much.

How do you know when your parents hate you?

The house catches on fire, and they send you inside to play.

• • •

What did the Jewish doctor tell the Arab who'd just taken an overdose of sleeping pills?

"Have a couple of drinks and get some rest."

• • •

Why do Polacks have arms?

So their fingers don't smell like armpits.

• • •

How do you know when you have a bad acne problem?

Your dog calls you Spot.

• • •

How do you know when there's something wrong with your local day-care center?

Your kid plays strip poker at bath time.

• • •

What's the definition of a consultant?

A guy who knows fifty ways to screw but doesn't know any women.

So the bride and groom check into a motel on their wedding night. They're both young and very inexperienced.

They have sex, like it so much they get it on again, and end up screwing six more times before dawn.

As they're drifting off to sleep, the bride screams and starts crying.

"What's the matter, honey?" the groom asks.

She points to his shriveled up dick and cries, "Here we are, married one night, and we're already used it all up!"

• • •

What makes a bull sweat?

A tight jersey.

• • •

What's worse than a stranger sneezing in your face?

When he wipes his nose on your sleeve.

• • •

How does a necrophiliac beat the heat?

He goes to the morgue and has a cold one.

• • •

How do you play baseball in Mexico?

Drink some water and try to make it home.

The mother takes her five-year-old kid to the sporting goods store and says to the man working there, "I want to buy a baseball mitt for my son. How much do they cost?"

The clerk says, "Sixty dollars."

"That's way too much," the mother says. "How much is that bat?"

"Five dollars," the clerk says.

"I'll take it," the mother says.

As he's wrapping it up, the clerk says to her, "How about a ball for the bat?"

"No thanks," the mother says. "But I'll go down on you for the mitt."

• • •

Why is a blow job like chewing gum?

It's tough getting rid of the wad when you're done.

• • •

How do you know when your secretary is truly honest?

She calls in lazy.

• • •

What's the definition of a singles bar?

A place where girls go to look for husbands . . . and husbands go to look for girls.

A Really Gross Variety

What's the difference between love and insan

Insanity lasts forever.

• • •

How do you know when you're in a dyke bar?

Even the pool table doesn't have any balls.

• • •

Why did the blonde stay in the car wash for three hours?

She thought it was raining too hard to drive.

• • •

Why did Israel win the Six Day War so fast?

The tanks were rented.

• • •

Why do Italian women spend so much time in beauty parlors?

The estimates take three hours.

• • •

Why did the Jew marry the girl born on February 29?

So he'd only have to buy her a present every four years.

Why did the Polish photographer start collecting burned-out lightbulbs?

He was building a darkroom.

• • •

How can you spot the redneck at Sea World?

He's the one carrying a fishing pole.

• • •

What happened when the nun got tired of using candles?

She called in an electrician.

• • •

An agent from the Internal Revenue Service goes to see an old lady to audit her tax returns for the last few years. As he's working, he notices a big bowl of almonds on her kitchen table.

He says to the old lady, "Mind if I have an almond?"

The old lady tells him, "Of course not, help yourself."

The auditor starts munching on the almonds as he's going over her tax returns. An hour later, he realizes that he's eaten all of them.

"I'm really sorry," he apologizes. "It's not bad enough I have to audit you, but then to eat all your almonds . . . I'm ashamed of myself."

"Oh, that's all right, sonny," the old lady says. "I already sucked all the chocolate off them."

A Really Gross Variety

So Harry is banging his best friend Sam's wife. Just as they're going at it hot and heavy, the phone rings.

The woman answers it, talks for a moment, then hangs up.

"That was Sam," she says.

"Shit!" Harry leaps out of the bed and starts grabbing his clothes.

"Don't worry," she says. "He just called to say he's out bowling with you."

• • •

Hear about the blind prostitute?

You really gotta hand it to her.

• • •

How do you know when a girl's really ugly?

She blindfolds herself before she takes a bath.

• • •

So the Polish judge says to the defendant, "You are charged with purse snatching. How do you plead, guilty or not guilty?"

"Not guilty," the defendant replies.

"Then what the hell are you doing here? Go home," the Polish judge tells him.

• • •

How many mice does it take to screw in a lightbulb?

Two, if they're small enough.

Why does the Pope shower in a bathing suit?

He doesn't like to look down on the unemployed.

• • •

How can you spot Dolly Parton's baby?

It's the one with stretch marks on his lips.

• • •

What's the definition of a lap dog?

A really ugly girl who gives blow jobs.

• • •

"And what was the extent of the defendant's involvement in this matter?" the judge asked the woman bringing suit in the paternity case.

She replied, "Oh, I guess about six and a half inches."

• • •

Mary comes home from her third date with a dreamy guy and is on cloud nine. She gleefully rips off her clothes and tosses them all over the bedroom before flopping into bed and falling asleep.

The next morning, her mother says to her, "So, did you have fun last night?"

"It was all right," Mary replies.

"It must have been better than that," her mother says. "Your panties are still stuck to the ceiling."

• • •

A Really Gross Variety

The Puerto Rican girl is on the witness stand. The prosecutor says to her, "When you were being raped, did you scream for help?"

The girl nods.

The prosecutor asks, "And did anyone come?"

The Puerto Rican girl nods again. "First he did, then I did."

• • •

What did the rooster say to the hen?

"How do you want your egg this morning?"

• • •

Why is sex with husbands like a soap opera?

It's over just as things are getting interesting.

• • •

How can you tell when you have bad breath?

You walk into the dentist's office and he goes for the laughing gas.

• • •

How do you know when you're really a loser?

A whore says to you, "Sorry, not on the first date."

• • •

How do you know when a nuclear power plant isn't safe?

The billing department moves out.

Why do so many black girls miss the first day of school?

Morning sickness.

• • •

Two Polish teenagers really want to lose their cherries, so they go to the local whorehouse. Because it's Saturday and the place is really crowded, they have to take turns with one whore.

The hooker beckons the first Polack into the room and hands him a rubber.

"Put this on," she says. "So I don't get pregnant."

The first Polack puts on the rubber and has sex with the hooker. When he's done, the second Polack goes into the room. The hooker hands him a rubber and says, "Put this on so I don't get pregnant."

A week later, the first Polack says to his friend, "Do you really care if that whore gets pregnant?"

"Hell no," the friend says.

"Me neither," the first Polack says. "Let's take these rubbers off."

• • •

What's the difference between garbage and an ugly girl?

Garbage gets picked up at least once a week.

• • •

Hear about the slutty cheerleader?

She came home from the football game with a bad case of athlete's fetus.

A Really Gross Variety

So Murray and Irving are sitting on a park bench in Miami Beach. Irving says to Murray, "I'm seventy years old, I've got two million in the bank, and I'm in love with a blonde who's half my age. Do you think she'd marry me if I told her I was only fifty?"

Murray tells his friend, "I think you'd do a lot better if you told her you were eighty."

• • •

Why is life like a cock?

When it's soft, it's hard to beat; when it's hard, you get screwed.

• • •

Why do men shake their peckers after taking a leak?

Because cocks can't *sniff.*

• • •

What's the best thing about contraceptive sponges?

After sex, women can wash dishes.

• • •

Jake is eighty years old. Dorothy is also eighty. They are having an affair in the nursing home. He goes into Dorothy's room every day and sits on her bed, where she takes his aging pecker in her hand and just holds it for an hour or so.

They do this for several months, then one day Jake doesn't show up in Dorothy's room. She waits until the next day, but he doesn't show. A week later, she hunts him down and asks him where he's been.

"I miss holding your cock in my hand," she tells him.

Jake confesses, "I've been seeing Mrs. Schwartz in room ten. She holds my cock much better."

Dorothy is furious. She asks Jake, "What has Mrs. Schwartz got that I haven't got?"

Jake responds, "Parkinson's disease."

• • •

What do you call ten feminists in a refrigerator?

Cold cunts.

• • •

"Daddy, daddy, what's a transvestite?"

"Shut up and unhook my bra!"

• • •

What do you call a virgin who just lost her cherry on a waterbed?

The Red Sea.

A Really Gross Variety

Hear about the new all-female delivery service?

It's called UPMS—they deliver whenever the fuck they feel like it.

• • •

So the old man walks into a whorehouse and says to the madam, "I want to get me laid. I hear tell you got lots of pretty ladies here."

The madam eyes the old man suspiciously and asks him, "Just how old are you, Pop?"

"Ninety-two."

"Ninety-two?" the madam exclaims. "Hell, Pop— you've already had it."

"Well then," the old man asks, reaching into his back pocket for his wallet, "how much do I owe you?"

• • •

Hear about the lovesick gynecologist?

He looked up an old girlfriend.

• • •

What's big and brown and lays in the woods?

Smokey the Hooker.

• • •

What do you get when you cross a Hell's Angel with a Jehovah's Witness?

Someone who knocks on your door early in the morning and tells you to go fuck yourself.

So the guy goes to the whorehouse. Once in the room with the blond hooker, he puts fifty dollars on the bed and drops his pants.

The hooker gasps—the guy's got an eighteen-inch cock.

She says, "I'm not putting that inside me! I'll lick it, I'll suck it, but that's all."

"Forget it," the guy says, taking back his fifty bucks. "I can do that myself."

● ● ●

What's black and hairy and fell off a wall?

Humpty Cunt.

● ● ●

What's the difference between eating sushi and eating pussy?

The rice.

● ● ●

How do blondes part their hair?

They spread their legs.

● ● ●

What do you call a dog with three legs?

Tippy.

● ● ●

A Really Gross Variety

Hear about the hooker who failed her driving test three times?

She couldn't remember to sit up straight in the front seat.

• • •

What's a Mexican whore's favorite drink?

A penis colada.

• • •

How many blondes does it take to make popcorn?

Three—one to hold the pot and two to shake the stove.

• • •

What do women and beer bottles have in common?

They're both empty from the neck up.

• • •

What do you get when you turn three blondes upside down?

Three brunettes.

• • •

What's the definition of uptight?

A chick who puts a rubber on her vibrator.

• • •

What are the three levels of sex for married couples?

1. House sex—you have sex in every room in the house.

2. Bedroom sex—you make love in the bedroom after the kids are asleep and all the shades are pulled down.

3. Hallway sex—you pass each other in the hallway and say, "Fuck you."

• • •

How do you use a rubber twice?

Turn it inside out and shake the fuck out of it.

• • •

The young virgin farmboy drives to the big city in search of a whorehouse. He finds one, and goes upstairs with a hooker. He explains that he's never been with a woman before.

The hooker says, "No problem, honey." She undresses him, then herself, and lies down on the bed. He crawls on top of her. The hooker says, "Okay, stick it in, honey . . . all the way . . . now pull it out . . . now put it back . . . now pull it out . . ."

"For Christ's sake," the farmboy says, "can't you make up your mind?"

• • •

A Really Gross Variety

The husband comes home early from work and finds his wife on all fours, scrubbing the floor. All she's wearing is panties. The husband can't resist—he gets down on all fours, yanks down her panties, and slips her the salami, screwing her good.

When he's finished, he smacks his wife on the side of the head.

"What did you do that for?" she asks, angry.

"For not looking to see who it was!" the husband replies.

• • •

Heard about the new Tempura House?

It's a halfway house for lightly battered women.

• • •

What's a girl's definition of a dilemma?

A guy with a ten-inch dick and herpes.

• • •

What do women and screen doors have in common?

The harder you bang them, the looser they get.

• • •

The traveling salesman stops at the farmhouse and asks the farmer for room and board for the night.

The farmer says, "We ain't got any empty rooms, mister, but you can sleep with my daughter if you promise not to disturb her."

The salesman agrees, and is taken upstairs to the daughter's room. He slips out of his clothes and gets into bed. He puts a hand on the daughter's thigh, and she doesn't protest. Emboldened now, the salesman puts a hand on her left breast, and still she does not protest. Going for broke, the salesman slips his pecker into the daughter and has a grand old time.

The next morning the farmer charges the salesman two dollars. "Only chargin' you half," the farmer explains, "seein' how you had to share the bed and such."

The salesman pays him and says, "Your daughter seemed very nice, sir, but she was sort of cold."

"She oughta be," the farmer replies. "We're burying her this afternoon."

• • •

The old lady walks into a bar. She's eighty if she's a day. She also has a pigeon on her shoulder. She announces to everyone, "Whoever guesses the weight of this pigeon can screw me."

A guy at the end of the bar calls out, "One thousand pounds."

The old lady replies, "Close enough."

• • •

A Really Gross Variety

What does a blonde do after sex?

Walk home.

• • •

What do you call a pimple on a Polish woman's ass?

A brain tumor.

• • •

So little Betsy comes home from school and starts asking her mother all sorts of questions. She asks, "Mommy, where did my baby brother come from?"

Her mother replies, "The stork brought him, Betsy."

Betsy asks, "And where did the twins from down the street come from?"

"The stork brought them, too," her mother says.

Little Betsy says, "Jesus Christ, doesn't anyone in this neighborhood fuck anymore?"

• • •

The Jewish businessman is being audited by the IRS. The tax man says, "You're deducting three thousand dollars for the birth of your baby. You can't do that, because she was born in January."

"True," says the Jewish guy, "but the work was done last year."

• • •

What do women and dog shit have in common?

The older they get, the easier they are to pick up.

What's the difference between a proctologist and a bartender?

The proctologist only has to look at one asshole at a time.

• • •

Hear about the stuck-up prostitute?

She was too good to go fuck herself.

• • •

Why can't women be trusted?

They bleed for four days and don't die.

• • •

What do you call an Ethiopian paratrooper?

Gone with the wind.

• • •

What's black and white and red all over?

South Africa.

• • •

What do you get when you cross a tropical fruit with a stripper?

A banana that peels itself.

• • •

A Really Gross Variety

Two construction workers, Al and Ted, are having a beer after work. Al asks Ted, "Hey, Ted, do you like women who don't shave their legs?"

Ted replies, "Nah, I hate women who don't shave their legs."

Al asks him, "Do you like women who never shave their armpits."

Ted says, "Nah, I hate women who don't shave their armpits."

"And do you like women who have big fat warts on the ends of their nose?"

"Nope."

"Then if you don't like women with hairy legs and armpits, and have warts on the ends of their nose," Al asks, "why the hell are you fucking my wife?"

• • •

What happened to the fly on the toilet seat?

It got pissed off.

• • •

What's the difference between a man and a bird?

A man doesn't eat with his pecker.

• • •

How do you know when a woman is really dumb?

She has to take off her bra to count to two.

• • •

How do you know when a woman is too old?

Her age and phone number are the same.

• • •

Then there was the baby that was so ugly, they threw her away and kept the afterbirth.

• • •

How do you know when a girl is really ugly?

Even the tide won't take her out.

• • •

So the Mother Superior was asking the girls in the convent what they wanted to do when they grew up.

A thirteen-year-old girl replied, "I want to be a prostitute!"

The Mother Superior got all red in the face and asked the girl, "Did I hear you correctly? Did you say you want to be a prostitute?"

"That's right."

"That's all right then," the Mother Superior told her. "I thought you said you wanted to be a Protestant!"

• • •

Old proverb: If God hadn't wanted us to eat pussy, He wouldn't have made them look like tacos.

• • •

A Really Gross Variety

Why doesn't Jesus Christ eat M&Ms?

They keep falling through the holes in his hands.

• • •

*Hear about the leper who worked as a male prosti-
tute?*

He was doing great until business fell off.

• • •

*What do you get when you cross a macho man and
a sensitive man?*

A gay trucker.

• • •

Why did the ugly girl take up jogging?

It was the only way she could hear heavy breathing.

• • •

How do you know when you're an unwanted baby?

Your bath toys are a toaster and a radio.

• • •

"My wife treats me like a god," Ben said to his friend
at the bar. "Every meal she cooks is a burnt offering."

• • •

A man is walking down the street when he meets God. He asks God, "Why did you make women so beautiful?"

God tells him, "So you will love them."

The man asks God, "Why did you make women so soft?"

"So you will love them," God says.

The man asks, "Why did you make women so stupid?"

God says, "So they will love you."

• • •

Why do only good girls keep diaries?

Bad girls don't have the time.

• • •

How do you trick a Polish woman into marrying you?

Tell her she is pregnant.

• • •

How do you know when you're living in Alabama?

You fart in public and blame it on your dog.

• • •

What's the nicest thing you can say to a girl from Alabama?

"Nice tooth."

• • •

A Really Gross Variety

How do you know when you're really in the South?

You go to a wedding reception at Denny's.

• • •

What's one definition of a loser?

A guy who gets blacklisted by a bowling alley.

• • •

So the woman calls the town psychiatrist and cries, "Doctor, you've got to come over right away. My husband's in really bad shape."

The shrink rushes over. The worried wife says, "Thank God you're here, Doctor. Just go down the hall. He's in the last room on the right."

The shrink goes into the room and sees the woman's husband sitting on the edge of the bathtub, dangling a fishing line in the toilet.

He goes back to the wife and says, "Yes, this is very serious. Why didn't you call me sooner?"

"Who had time?" the wife asks. "I've been cleaning fish all week."

• • •

What did one dog say to the other dog when they saw a parking meter for the first time?

"Look, Rover—a pay toilet."

• • •

What's a mixed marriage in San Francisco?

Partners of the opposite sex.

• • •

So six-year-old Billy says to his best friend Andy, "My daddy has two dicks."

"Have you seen 'em?" Andy asks.

"Sure," Billy says. "He uses one to pee with and the other to brush the baby-sitter's teeth."

• • •

What's the definition of alimony?

A man's cash surrender value.

• • •

What's the difference between a dog and a dick?

A dog stops coming when you beat it.

• • •

Where does virgin wool come from?

Really ugly sheep.

• • •

How do you know when you're from Georgia?

Your car breaks down on the side of the road and you never go back to get it.

• • •

A Really Gross Variety

What's another way of knowing you're from Georgia?

You think people who have electricity are snobs.

• • •

What's another?

You know how to milk a goat.

• • •

Why do dogs stick their noses in blondes' crotches?

Because they can.

• • •

What's the difference between two lawyers in a BMW and a porcupine?

A porcupine has his pricks on the outside.

• • •

Why was the ninety-year-old man acquitted of rape?

The evidence wouldn't stand up in court.

• • •

Two Polacks are standing on the street corner, watching a dog lick his balls.

"I sure wish I could do that," the first Polack says.

"You better ask the dog first," the second Polack says.

• • •

…icks count to ten?

*o . . . three . . . then another . . . then
."*

• • •

*What's the best thing about having a female presi-
dent?*

You don't have to pay the bitch as much as a man.

• • •

*Hear about the Polack who went ice fishing and came
home with twenty pounds of ice?*

His wife died trying to fry it.

• • •

*What did Helen Keller say when she picked up a
matzo?*

"This is good. Who wrote this?"

• • •

"Grandpa, Grandpa," little Joey says. "Can you
croak like a frog?"

"I guess so," Grandpa says. "Why do you ask?"

"Cause Mommy says that when you croak, we're
all going to Disney World!"

• • •

So the gay guy checks into the hospital to have an operation. The morning after, the surgeon goes to see the patient.

"So how are you doing this morning?" the surgeon asks.

"Okay, Doctor. I just have one question: When can I . . . you know . . . resume a normal sex life?"

"I'm not sure," the surgeon says. "You're the first one to ask after a tonsillectomy."

• • •

What's the definition of "indefinitely"?

You're indefinitely when your balls are slapping her ass.

• • •

So the gynecologist came home from work and slumped into a chair.

"Tired, dear?" his wife asked.

"Honey, I'm bushed."

• • •

Why is aspirin white?

Because it works.

• • •

How do you make a woman scream twice?

Fuck her up the ass then wipe your dick on her blouse.

"Mommy, Mommy," little Joey asks. "Where do babies come from?"

"The stork," Mommy says.

"I know," Joey says. "But who fucks the stork?"

• • •

What does NRA really stand for?

Nigger Removal Agency.

• • •

What do you get when you cross an agnostic and a Jehovah's Witness?

Someone who knocks on your door for no reason.

• • •

What's the difference between a Polish woman and a catfish?

One has whiskers and smells bad. The other one is a fish.

• • •

Why don't Bosnians go out to bars anymore?

They get bombed at home.

• • •

So the Polack leaves the bar drunk out of his mind. Despite the bartender's protests, the Polack tries to drive home.

Less than a mile away, he gets pulled over by a cop.

"What seems to be the problcm, occifer?" the Polack asks the cop drunkenly.

"Good evening, sir," the cop says. "Drinking?"

The Polack says, "You buying?"

• • •

"Doctor," Epstein says, "my wife is driving me crazy. I have to get rid of her. What can I do?"

"Take these pills," the doctor says. "Give her one a day then screw her six times. In a month it will kill her."

A month later, Epstein shows up in the doctor's office in a wheelchair, looking thirty years older.

"My God," the doctor exclaims. "What happened to you?"

"It's okay, Doc," Epstein says. "In another two days she'll be dead."

• • •

Why do men have bigger brains than dogs?

So they don't hump women's legs at parties.

• • •

What does a faggot get after he's been gang-raped?

A full moon.

• • •

What does Sinead O'Connor do after she combs her hair?

Pulls her pants up.

• • •

What's the difference between a Jewish American Princess and a pit bull?

A nose job and a mink coat.

2

SO
GROSS
EVEN
WE
WERE
OFFENDED

• • • • • •

What do the Unabomber and a girl from Alabama have in common?

They were both fingered by their brother.

• • •

What company is the leading manufacturer of vibrators?

Genital Electric.

• • •

What do you call a man who has sex with rabbits?

Elmer Fuck.

• • •

How do you know when your girlfriend is getting too fat?

The guy from Prudential offers her group insurance.

• • •

What's the definition of old age?

When all the girls in your little black book are grandmothers.

Another definition of old age: When not only can't you cut the mustard, you can't even open the jar.

• • •

What did one alligator say to the other alligator after the ValueJet crash in the Everglades?

"Not bad for airline food."

• • •

Why did the Polish burglar break two windows?

One to get in, one to get out.

• • •

How did the Polish dog get a flat nose?

Chasing parked cars.

• • •

What's the easiest way to get into a sex club?

Just come.

• • •

Why did the girl stop dating the cannibal?

He just wanted her for her body.

• • •

What's the definition of Italian ices?

A frozen cesspool.

So Gross Even We Were Offended

How do you know when you have a bad physician?

His office plants are dead.

• • •

How many Arab terrorists does it take to screw in a lightbulb?

None—they just stand around and threaten it.

• • •

What was the first lie ever told?

Adam to Eve: "Eat this apple. It'll make your tits bigger."

• • •

Why are old men like babies?

They like to be Pampered.

• • •

What do you call diapers for old people?

Grampers.

• • •

What's the difference between a slut and a toothbrush?

You don't let your friends borrow your toothbrush.

• • •

Why don't fat dykes wear yellow?

So they won't be mistaken for taxicabs.

• • •

Why are men like microwaves?

They get hot really fast, then go off in thirty seconds.

• • •

What's the definition of a dyke?

A woman trying to do a man's work.

• • •

Two drunken Polacks come stumbling out of a bar and start pissing in a garden. A cop comes along and starts writing them each a ticket for public urination.

The cop, writing up the ticket, says to the first Polack, "Where do you live?"

The first Polack is so drunk, he can't remember. He tells the cop, "I don't know."

Exasperated, the cop says to the second Polack, "Where do *you* live?"

The second Polack says proudly, "I live next door to him."

• • •

So Gross Even We Were Offended

A tourist couple walk into a bar in a really tough Irish neighborhood in New York's Hell's Kitchen.

The wife says to her husband, "Look, Sidney—there's sawdust on the floor. How quaint!"

"That ain't sawdust, lady," the bartender says, "That's last night's furniture."

• • •

What do you call a black woman with two or more daughters?

The madam.

• • •

Why did the prostitute stop giving blow jobs and become a computer programmer?

There was less downtime.

• • •

So the eighty-year-old man is prouder than hell when his twenty-year-old wife gets pregnant.

Nine months to the day, she is rushed to the maternity ward. A few hours later, the nurse comes out and says to the old man, "Congratulations, sir. Your wife just had twins."

The old man says to the nurse, "It just goes to show you—there may be snow on the roof, but there's fire in the furnace!"

"Then you better change your filters," the nurse tells the old man, "because both babies are black."

• • •

What's the best thing about having Alzheimer's disease?

You can hide your own Easter eggs.

• • •

What are the last three words any man wants to hear when he's making love?

"Darling, I'm home."

• • •

You know a girl is ugly when . . .

. . . The welcome wagon burns a cross on her lawn.

. . . The neighborhood Peeping Tom pulls *down* her shade.

. . . She has her face capped.

. . . She wins a malpractice suit—against her parents.

. . . She leaves the beauty parlor and they ask her to use the back door.

• • •

How does an eighty-year-old man spell "sex"?

H-E-L-P.

• • •

So the husband says to the divorce judge, "I came home, your honor, and I found my wife in bed with a strange man."

"What did she say?" the judge asked.

"That's what bothers me the most," the husband replies. "She said, 'Well, look who's home. The old blabbermouth. Now the whole neighborhood will know!' "

• • •

"I hear you advertised for a wife," Frank said to Bob.

"Yeah," Bob replies.

"Get a response?" Franks wants to know.

"Hundreds of them," Bob says. "They all said, 'Take mine.' "

• • •

The man wakes up in a hospital, groggy.

"Where am I?" he asks an intern.

The intern says, "You had a terrible accident and you're in the hospital. Do you want the good news or the bad news first?"

"It can't be any worse than I feel, so give me the bad news first."

"The bad news is we had to operate. The surgeons amputated both of your feet."

"That's awful. What's the good news?"

"The good news is, the guy in the next bed wants to buy your shoes."

• • •

Then there was the loser who called the suicide hot-line.

They told him he was doing the right thing.

• • •

Hear about the girl who got her good looks from her father?

He was a plastic surgeon.

• • •

Hear about the schizophrenic's bathroom?

The towels were marked "His" and "His."

• • •

Hear about the really ugly girl?

Her gynecologist would only examine her by mail.

• • •

What's the best thing about getting a blow job?

The five minutes of silence.

• • •

"I don't understand," Joe complained to his friend. "People take an instant dislike to me the moment I tell them I'm a lawyer. Why is that?"

"Maybe it just saves time."

• • •

This truck driver was speeding through a small country town and ran over a big rooster. He appeared at the first farm he came to and knocked on the door. A farmer's wife answered. "What do you want?" she asked.

"Ma'am," the trucker said, "I would like to replace your rooster."

The farmer's wife looked him up and down. "Let me see your manhood, mister," she said.

The truck driver was confused, but showed her his pecker.

"Fair enough," the farmer's wife replied. "The chickens are out back."

• • •

What's the difference between politics and a wife?

Politics suck.

• • •

How do you know you're really getting old?

There are twelve candles on your piece of birthday cake.

• • •

What do you call a black woman who practices birth control?

A humanitarian.

• • •

The lonely secretary is walking home from work one day when she spots a strange-looking bottle on the side of the road. She picks it up and dusts it off, unleashing a genie.

"I grant you one wish," the genie says.

The homely girl thinks about it. She says to the genie, "I'm a virgin. When I get home, I'd like to see my cat turned into a handsome young hunky guy."

"So shall it be," the genie booms and disappears back into the bottle.

The secretary rushes home and finds a tall, handsome stud in her apartment. He rips her clothes off and carries her into the bedroom, laying her on the bed. He kisses her and nuzzles her neck until she's ready to explode with passion.

"Oh, take me, take me now," she gasps.

"I would, but you had me neutered last month."

• • •

What do you call diarrhea in Mississippi?

A brain drain.

• • •

Why are peckers like Calvin Klein jeans?

It takes a lot of yanks to get them off.

• • •

When a Puerto Rican leaves the United States, he says, "Farewell." When he comes back, he says, "Welfare."

Why did the eighty-year-old woman stop wearing her belt?

Every time she tried to tighten it, her tits got in the way.

• • •

What's the definition of a meat substitute?

A dildo made from soybeans.

• • •

Bill Gates and Steven Spielberg have lunch together at a fancy Beverly Hills bistro. Afterwards, they're walking along Rodeo Drive and pass a Rolls-Royce dealership.

Bill Gates inspects the sticker on the window of one Rolls and says, "Seventy-five grand. I think I'll buy it."

"No, let me, Bill," Spielberg says. "You paid for lunch."

• • •

Two men are on death row, scheduled to die on the same night. The warden asks each one if he has any last requests.

The first inmate says, "Yes, Warden. I'd like to hear 'Achy Breaky Heart' one last time before I die."

The warden says to the second inmate, "Do you have a last request?"

"Yes. Kill me first."

• • •

Hear about the Newt Gingrich bucket meal at Kentucky Fried Chicken?

It's full of right wings and assholes.

• • •

So the lady calls the local police station and declares, "Officer, there's a Democrat masturbating in the window of the apartment across the alley!"

The cop asks her, "Lady, how do you know it's a Democrat?"

The lady says, "If it was a Republican, he'd be out screwing somebody!"

• • •

"So," the sportscaster asks the coach of the losing Miami Dolphins, "what do you think of your team's execution?"

The coach replies, "I'm all for it."

• • •

How do you know when you're really a slob?

There are more dishes in your sink than in your cabinet.

• • •

What's the definition of a total loser?

A guy who loses his wife in a poker game.

• • •

Joe and Ed are having beers at their local tavern.

Ed asks his friend, "So how was your blind date last night?"

Joe replies, "It was terrible. We had a nice dinner, then we drank some wine and sat down on the couch and started kissing. She seduced me and we made passionate love."

"What's so terrible about that?"

Joe says, "After we were done, she asked me to light her cigar."

• • •

What's another definition of a total loser?

Someone who wins first prize in a fart-off.

• • •

How do you know when your kid's a pervert?

He plays with the dog and dresses up like a fire hydrant.

• • •

What's the definition of Branson, Missouri?

Las Vegas for the toothless.

• • •

Why aren't niggers ever blond?

They're dumb enough without it.

• • •

Why are blondes like computers?

You don't appreciate them until they go down.

• • •

What's the definition of a legal secretary?

A chick that's over eighteen.

• • •

Why do women fart after they piss?

They can't shake it, so they blow-dry it.

• • •

Why do farts smell?

So deaf people can enjoy them, too.

• • •

A man goes to a seedy hotel room with a prostitute. He's a little nervous, so he asks her, "Have you ever been picked up by the fuzz?"

"No," the whore says, "but if that's what you want, it'll cost you an extra fifty bucks."

• • •

What do you call a leper in a bathtub?

Stew.

• • •

So Gross Even We Were Offended

The Polish woman calls the fire department and cries, "Hurry, our house is burning down!"

"Okay, lady," the fire chief says. "Just calm down and tell us how to get there."

The Polish woman responds, "Dammit, take that big red truck!"

• • •

The Polish kid was walking down the street and almost stepped in a pile of dog shit.

So delighted was he with his luck, he scooped up a handful of the dog shit and ran home. He burst into the house and said proudly to his father, "Look, Pa, what I almost stepped in!"

• • •

Why did the Polack stop moving his bowels?

He was afraid he'd forget where he put them.

• • •

So Epstein says to his physician, "Doctor, I've got five penises."

"My God! How do your pants fit?" the doctor asks him.

"Like a glove," Epstein says.

• • •

What do you give an elephant with diarrhea?

Lots of room.

Why do deaf women masturbate with only one hand?

So they can moan with the other.

• • •

Moses comes back from Mount Sinai and says to the Jews, "I've got good news and bad news. The good news is, I got the Twelve Commandments knocked down to Ten Commandments. The bad news is, adultery is still in."

• • •

When Mrs. Hepplewhite goes to see her gynecologist, he helps her onto the table, then asks, "So what seems to be the problem?"

Mrs. Hepplewhite says, "Ever since you fitted me with that diaphragm, I've been pissing purple."

"My God!" the doc exclaims. "What kind of jelly are you using?"

"Welch's Grape," she tells him.

• • •

What's a transvestite's idea of a good time?

To eat, drink, and be Mary.

3

IN A WORD, SEX

● ● ● ● ● ● ●

Why is an impotent man like a Christmas tree?

The balls of both are for show.

• • •

Why did Woody Allen go to see his physician?

He had diaper rash.

• • •

Why did the old lady piss all over her husband?

To celebrate their golden wedding anniversary.

• • •

For their fiftieth wedding anniversary, Harry and Gertrude returned to the hotel where they'd spent their honeymoon.

As they got ready for bed, Gertrude decided to put on the see-through two hundred dollar nightie she'd bought for the occasion. Only after she'd undressed did she realize that she'd left the nightie in the bathroom.

Stark naked, she tiptoed over to get it. Harry, who had taken off his glasses, looked at his wife and said, "For God's sake, Gertrude. For two hundred dollars they could've at least ironed it!"

Three secretaries discovered that they all had boy-friends with the same name—Stanley.

To avoid confusion, they decided to nickname the men after different sodas.

The first secretary said, "I'll name mine 7-Up, because he's got seven inches and it's always up."

The second secretary said, "I'll name mine Mountain Dew, because he loves my mountains and he sure can do it."

The third secretary said, "I'll name mine Wild Turkey."

"You can't do that," the first one says. "That's not a soda, it's a hard liquor."

"So is he," the third one replies.

• • •

Why are Peace Corps workers like plastic surgeons?

They both specialize in underdeveloped areas.

• • •

How many men does it take to screw in a lightbulb?

One—men will screw anything.

• • •

Why are tampons so popular all over the world?

They keep the Reds in, the Poles out, the Greeks happy, and the French hungry.

• • •

In a Word, Sex

A trucker stops for lunch on I-95. He starts eyeballing the really good-looking waitress. She leans over to take his order, shoving her huge tits in his face.

"What would you like, sugar?" she says to him.

"I'd love a little pussy," he replies.

"So would I!" the waitress exclaims. "Mine's really huge."

• • •

Why don't most men care if women shave their pussies?

They don't mind going through the bush to get to the picnic.

• • •

What's green and smells like pork?

Kermit's finger.

• • •

What do you get when you cross an anteater and a vibrator?

An armadildo.

• • •

Heard about the new male birth control pill?

Take it the day after and it changes your blood type.

• • •

Morris, on his eightieth birthday, decides to fulfill a lifelong dream and go to a nudist colony.

No sooner does he sign in and shed his clothes than a gorgeous blonde comes over and gives him the best blow job of his life. Morris rushes back to the office and signs up for a year.

Walking around, he drops his cigar and bends over to pick it up. Before he can, a faggot dicks him up the butt.

Morris returns to the office and demands his money back.

"What happened?" the owner says. "I thought you were having a good time."

"Listen," Morris says. "I get excited once a month, but I drop my cigar five times a day!"

• • •

What's more boring than listening to a speech by Al Gore?

Watching Tipper undress.

• • •

Why did the necrophiliac cremate his girlfriend?

He wanted a piece of ash.

• • •

The sexaholic tells his psychiatrist, "I have a wife, a mistress, and four girlfriends. I love every type of sex there is, and I also love to jerk off and have wet dreams."

The shrink says to him, "Which type of sex do you love the best?"

He replies, "Masturbation. It feels good and you meet a much better class of people."

• • •

The young hooker reports for work on her first day at the whorehouse.

The madam says to her, "Do you have any questions?"

The hooker asks, "Yes. I was wondering how long dicks should be sucked."

The madam replies, "The same as the short ones, honey."

• • •

Hear about the Polish grandmother who went on the pill?

She didn't want any more grandchildren.

• • •

Then there's the flea who suffered from insomnia.

He only slept in snatches.

• • •

What do the president of Tupperware and a walrus have in common?

They both like a tight seal.

• • •

The deaf guy gets married and says to his new bride, "If you want sex and I'm asleep, just yank my dick twice."

"What if I don't feel like having sex?" his bride asks.

The deaf guy replies, "Then yank my cock fifty or sixty times."

• • •

Why is a cucumber better than a man?

Cucumbers stay hard for a whole week.

• • •

How do they define safe sex in Montana?

Branding the sheep that kick.

• • •

What's a politician's idea of safe sex?

No press.

• • •

A couple checks into the most expensive hotel in Paris. They order up room service—a cozy dinner for two. The room service waiter sets out the meal, then asks, "Will there be anything else?"

The husband replies, "No, thank you."

The waiter asks, "And for your wife?"

The husband thinks for a moment and says, "Yes. Call her and tell her I'll be home the day after tomorrow."

• • •

"I don't think my wife loves me anymore," the worried husband says to his shrink.

"How can you tell?" the shrink asks.

"Well, when I come home from work, she greets me at the door with a nice dry martini. Then she cooks me a great dinner. Later, when we go to bed, she lets me do all kinds of kinky things to her and she never objects."

"So what's the problem?"

"Maybe I'm being overly sensitive, but when she thinks I'm asleep, she whispers in my ear, 'Die, you lousy son of a bitch, die!' "

• • •

What do you call a rock star with PMS?

John Cougar Menstrual-cramp.

• • •

Two old men are sitting in Central Park. Max says to Sam, "So congratulate me. I'm getting married again."

"Married? Max are you crazy? You're ninety-two years old."

"So sue me, I'm in love."

"Can she cook?" Sam wants to know.

"She can't even boil water."

"Is she pretty at least?" Sam asks.

"She's got a face like a horse."

"Is she, maybe, good in bed?"

"Good in bed?" Max snorts. "She's two years older than me and hasn't done it in thirty years."

"Then why the hell are you marrying her?"

"She can drive at night."

• • •

What's the difference between oral sex and Christmas?

At Christmas, it's better to give than to receive.

• • •

Why wasn't Heidi Fleiss handcuffed when she was arrested by the L.A. police?

It would have cost an extra $500.

• • •

The wife of a Hell's Angel goes to see a fortune teller.

"Prepare to be a widow," the fortune teller says, gazing into her crystal ball. "Your old man is going to die very, very soon."

"Yeah, I know. But will I be acquitted?"

• • •

A tourist gets lost in the back woods of Alabama. He comes upon a broken-down mobile home out in the middle of nowhere. Two rednecks are sitting in lawn chairs out front. The tourist asks them directions back to the interstate. They tell him. Before he leaves, though, he asks one of the rednecks, "What do you boys do for fun out here?"

"Well," the first redneck says, "mostly what we do for fun is hunt and kill and fuck."

"What do you hunt and kill?"

"Something to fuck."

• • •

Two old whores are watching a parade. The first one starts to cheer and wave the American flag.

"I just love soldiers," she says.

"Yeah, yeah," her friend says. "You say that every war."

• • •

The old geezer says to his physician, "Doc, I just don't have any interest in sex anymore."

The doctor asks, "How old are you, Jake?"

Old Jake replies, "Ninety-six."

The doctor tells him, "Exactly. Face it, Jake, you're not getting any younger. At your age, a man's bound to see a decrease in his sexual drive. When did you first notice that you were losing interest in sex?"

Jake says, "Twice last night, and then again this morning."

• • •

A worried husband says to the psychiatrist, "Doctor, I don't know what to do. My wife thinks she's a lawn mower!"

"That's terrible," the psychiatrist says. "Why didn't you bring her to see me sooner?"

"I tried, but my neighbor wouldn't return her."

• • •

On the night of her wedding, the young bride pulled her mother aside and asked her, "Mama, tell me how to make my new husband happy."

Her mother replies, "Well, when two people love each other, they make love."

"Oh, I know all about fucking, Mama," the bride said. "I want to know how to make lasagna."

• • •

Twelve-year-old Timmy comes home from school. His mother asks him, "Did you learn anything today?"

Timmy says, "We learned all about sex education. About penises and vaginas and stuff."

Timmy's mother is shocked. She says, "Is that what they're teaching you in school nowadays? I'm going to complain to the principal!"

"Relax, Mom," Timmy assures her. "This is the nineties. It's all a part of what they call higher education."

Timmy goes up to his room. An hour or so later, his mother calls him down to dinner. When he doesn't respond, she goes upstairs to his room. Timmy is lying on his bed, jerking off.

"Timmy, when you're done with your homework, supper's on the table."

• • •

Two perverts were watching a movie in a dark movie theater. When Demi Moore appeared on the screen, the first pervert said to the other, "I've had her, you know."

A few minutes later, Julia Roberts appeared on the screen. The first pervert said to the second pervert, "You know, I've had her, too."

Later, Melanie Griffith appeared on the screen. The second pervert said to his friend, "I suppose you had her, too?"

"Shhh," the first pervert replied. "I'm having her now."

• • •

So this man is having a vasectomy. During the delicate operation, one of his testicles falls onto the floor, and before the nurse can pick it up, the doctor steps on it.

The doctor tells the nurse, "Don't worry, we can replace it. Get me a very small onion." She does, and the doctor replaces the missing ball with the onion.

A few weeks later, the patient stops by to see the doctor, who asks him what seems to be the problem.

"Well, it's like this," the patient replies. "Every time I take a piss, my eyes water. Every time I come, I get heartburn. And every time I pass a Burger King, I get a hard-on!"

• • •

Why do women in Canada use hockey pucks instead of tampons?

They last three periods.

• • •

What do you get when you cross a prostitute and a pit bull?

The last blow job you'll ever get.

• • •

What's the difference between a penis and a paycheck?

You don't have to beg your wife to blow your paycheck.

So the guy walks into a singles bar and picks out the prettiest girl he an find. Sitting down next to her, he reaches into his pocket and pulls out a box. Inside the box is a small frog.

"He's really cute," the blonde says. "Does he do tricks?"

"He sure does," the guy says. "He eats pussy."

The blonde is skeptical, so the guy convinces her to return to his apartment to prove to her that his pet frog does, indeed, eat pussy. The blonde gets undressed and gets on the bed, spreading her legs. The guy puts the frog down between her legs, but the frog doesn't budge. The blonde says, "Well?"

"Okay, moron," the guy says to the frog. "I'm only going to show you one more time."

• • •

Norman walked into the neighborhood saloon and announced that he was divorcing his wife. The bartender asked why.

"Well," Norman said, "yesterday was her birthday, so I took her to the fanciest restaurant in town."

"So?" the bartender asked.

"So I order a bottle of their best champagne, and I made her a toast—'to the best woman a man could have.' "

"What's wrong with that?"

"Three of the waiters joined in."

• • •

"My wife would make a great soccer goalie," one man said to his friend. "I haven't scored in months."

• • •

"I knew the honeymoon was over," the same man said to his friend, "when I started going out every Thursday night with the boys."
"What's wrong with that?"
"So did she."

• • •

Hear about the woman who worked at a sperm bank and got pregnant?

She was arrested for embezzlement.

• • •

What's hairy and sucks blood?

Cunt Dracula.

• • •

"I'm sorry to say," the doctor said to the man, "that after examining your wife, we've discovered that she has acute angina."
"I know," her husband said, "but what's wrong with her?"

• • •

What do you call an anorexic with a yeast infection?

A quarter-pounder with cheese.

In a Word, Sex

So the doctor says to Ed, "You have a rare disease. The only thing that can cure you is fresh breast milk."

Ed advertises for a wet nurse. A beautiful woman responds to his ad and agrees to wet-nurse him. Their first time, Ed is happily sucking away and is pretty good at it, so much so that the wet nurse finds herself becoming aroused.

Feeling Ed sucking her tit, she moans, "Is there anything else I can do for you?"

"You wouldn't have any chocolate chip cookies, would you?" Ed asks.

• • •

Question: If girls are made of sugar and spice, why do they taste like anchovies?

• • •

So Bill's wife was in a terrible car accident and is in intensive care. Bill rushes to the hospital, where the doctor tells him, "Research shows that oral sex speeds a patient's recovery. I suggest you try it. I'll instruct the nurses to leave you both alone for the next hour."

Five minutes later, buzzers and bells bring doctors and nurses to the room. The doctors work furiously to save Bill's wife. When she is stabilized, the doctor asks him, "What went wrong?"

"I don't know," Bill replies. "I think she choked."

• • •

Two Polish fags meet in a gay bar and go home together. They spend the night butt-fucking and sucking each other off.

The next morning, one of the Polish fags gets dressed to leave. He extends his hand to the other Polish fag for a handshake.

"Are you crazy?" the second Polish fag exclaims. "I heard you can get AIDS that way!"

• • •

The residents of the small Southern town urge the sheriff to arrest the local homosexual. Seems he's been propositioning all the teenaged boys in town.

The sheriff dutifully arrests the fag and says to him, "Okay, homo. You got fifteen minutes to blow this town!"

The homosexual says, "I'll need at least two hours."

4

GROSS ETHNIC JOKES

● ● ● ● ● ● ●

Hear about the Jewish American Princess with lep-rosy?

She talked her head off.

• • •

What about the Puerto Rican who was too young to drive?

He stole taxis.

• • •

What's the difference between an Irishman and a Muslim?

An Irishman gets stoned before he sleeps with some-one else's wife.

• • •

What did the guy do after his Italian wife left him?

He masturbated with a Brillo pad.

• • •

How did the Jewish American Princess commit sui-cide?

She jumped off her credit cards.

How ugly was the Italian girl?

Even a leech wouldn't give her a hickey.

• • •

What's the definition of a virgin in Harlem?

A girl whose mother is too ugly to have a boyfriend.

• • •

How do Polish women remove their makeup?

With Easy-Off.

• • •

What is JAP aerobics?

Shopping faster.

• • •

How can you spot a JAP at an orgy?

She's the one who says, "What, my turn again?"

• • •

How can you spot the Italian parents at a PTA meeting?

They're the ones attending under an assumed name.

• • •

Gross Ethnic Jokes

How can you tell when a woman is half Irish and half Italian?

She mashes potatoes with her feet.

• • •

What does a Polish girl put behind her ears to attract men?

Her knees.

• • •

Why do Mexicans eat refried beans?

So they can get a second wind.

• • •

Why did the Irishman like to drink and drive?

He ran into the most interesting people.

• • •

How can you spot the WASP kid in the playground?

He's the one making mudpies with a Cuisinart.

• • •

So the Polish woman was allergic to birth control pills. She asked her gynecologist to recommend the best contraceptives.

The doctor said, "Try withdrawal, douches, and rubbers."

Three years later, the Polish woman was walking down the street with three children when she ran into her gynecologist, who said to her, "I see you didn't take my advice."

"I tried," the Polish woman said. "Stan here was a pullout, Stosh was a washout, and Vladimir was a blowout."

• • •

Hear about the black kid who got promoted to the second grade?

He was so excited, he cut himself shaving.

• • •

What's made out of metal and glass and comes in 5,000 pieces?

A car in Belfast.

• • •

Why did the Polack marry his dog?

Because he had to.

• • •

How do you keep a Polack from biting his nails?

Make him wear shoes.

Why are Catholic girls so quiet during sex?

They don't believe in talking to strangers.

• • •

Hear about the Polish duck hunters?

The decoy got away.

• • •

So a Jewish guy took his wife on a camping trip. As they sat around the campfire one night, a huge animal burst into the clearing. The Jew and his wife started running away. The wife cried out, "What the hell is it, a bear?"

The Jew, five yards ahead of his wife, yelled back, "How should I know? I'm in textiles, not furs!"

• • •

What do you get when you cross an Irishman with a German?

Someone who's too drunk to follow orders.

• • •

Hear about the Polish athlete?

He'd give his right arm to be ambidextrous.

• • •

Hear about the Klansman from Alabama?

He was a real sheethead.

Why did the Irish cancel St. Patrick's Day?

They dug him up and discovered he died from AIDS.

• • •

Why don't cannibals eat Jewish kids?

They're always spoiled.

• • •

Why are turtleneck sweaters so popular in Poland?

They hide the flea collars.

• • •

Hear about the Polack who won the lottery?

He bought a Winnebago with a wine cellar.

• • •

Hear about the new dance club in Israel?

It's called "Let My People Go-Go."

• • •

Where do black folks buy toys for their children?

FAO Schwartze.

• • •

So this black guy walks into a saloon accompanied by a big gorilla. The black guy says to the bartender, "Gimme two beers."

The bartender takes one look at the gorilla and says to the black guy, "Get the hell out of here. I don't serve gorillas in this place."

The black guy goes home, taking the gorilla with him. Once there, he shaves all the fur off the gorilla, then dresses the animal in a tight red dress and high heels.

The black guy goes back to the bar with the gorilla. He says to the bartender, "Gimme two beers."

The bartender gives the black guy two beers. The black guy takes the beers and, with the gorilla, goes to a table in the back.

The bartender says to a friend, "Ain't it always the case? A beautiful Italian girl walks in, and she's with a nigger."

• • •

Why did the Polish scientist stay up night after night?

He was trying to find a cure for insomnia.

• • •

Why is teen sex in Bosnia so exciting?

You never now if the car is going to explode before you do.

What do you call a fag from Tokyo?

A Japansie.

• • •

What do you call the alphabet in Harlem?

The impossible dream.

• • •

What's the difference between a Polish woman and a mosquito?

A mosquito stops sucking when you bash its head in.

• • •

What's the difference between Martin Luther King Day and St. Patrick's Day?

On St. Patrick's Day, people *want* to be Irish.

• • •

Who was the one man missing from the Million Man March?

The auctioneer.

• • •

What's black, three miles long, and smelly?

The line at the welfare office.

• • •

Gross Ethnic Jokes

What did the Polack say when he found a milk carton in the grass?

"Look—a cow's nest!"

• • •

What do you call a Polack with half a brain?
Gifted.

• • •

Why wasn't the Polack worried when his car was stolen?

He got the license plate number.

• • •

What did the Polish mother say when her daughter said she was pregnant?

"Don't worry, honey. Maybe it's not yours."

• • •

Why did the Polish woman take swimming lessons?
She wanted to be a hooker in Venice.

• • •

What's one job they don't have in Poland?
Mind reader.

• • •

Why couldn't the Polack get a job as the town idiot?

He was overqualified.

· · ·

Hear about the black guy who suffered from insomnia?

He kept waking up every few days.

· · ·

What's the most popular booth at the Polish carnival?

"Guess Your Age—$1.00."

· · ·

What is the ASPCA?

A Mexican singles bar.

· · ·

Hear about the Polish sky diver?

He was killed when his snorkel and flippers failed to open.

· · ·

Hear about the new Polish parachute?

It opens on impact.

· · ·

Gross Ethnic Jokes

How do you make a WASP laugh on Monday?

Tell him a joke on Friday.

• • •

The Polish airliner was in trouble. "Mayday, may-day," the pilot radioed to the tower.

"You're cleared to land," the radar tower came back. "Can you give us your height and position?"

"Well," the Polish pilot replies, "I'm five foot nine and I'm sitting in the front of the plane."

• • •

Hear about the Greek and the Polack who jumped off the Empire State Building?

The Greek guy was killed. The Polack got lost.

• • •

What do most of the patients in Irish hospitals have in common?

They were all IRA explosives experts.

• • •

What's the best way to grow dope?

Plant a Polack.

• • •

A man walks out of a house in Belfast. Another man walks up to him and sticks a gun to his head, saying, "Are you a Catholic or a Protestant?"

The first guy is afraid of getting shot if he says the wrong thing. He says, "As a matter of fact, I'm neither. I'm Jewish."

The gunman says, "Hell, I must be the luckiest Arab in Belfast tonight!"

• • •

A Catholic goes to confession. He says to the priest, "Bless me, Father, for I have sinned. I had sex with a married woman."

"That is a very bad sin," the priest says. "You must tell me who she was."

"I can't do that, Father," the man replies. "It wouldn't be right."

"Was it Mary Stevens?"

"No."

"Was it Patty Phillips?"

The man shakes his head. "Please, Father, don't make me tell."

"If you won't tell me, then you will have to do penance. Ten Hail Marys and fifty Our Fathers."

The priest sends him away. Outside, the man spots his friend, who asks him, "Did you tell him?"

"Yes."

"What did you get?"

"Ten Hail Marys, fifty Our Fathers, and a couple of great leads."

• • •

Gross Ethnic Jokes

Why did doctors stop circumcising black babies?

They were throwing away the best part.

• • •

What is Preparation H?

Toothpaste for Polacks.

• • •

Why aren't Jewish American Princesses ever attacked by sharks?

Professional courtesy.

• • •

Why are elephants and Jewish mothers alike?

Neither one ever forgets.

• • •

What would you call Mike Tyson if he had no arms or legs?

"Hey, nigger . . ."

• • •

What do black men and sperm have in common?

Only one in two million works.

• • •

How do they advertise BMWs in Harlem?

"You stole the radio—now steal the car!"

Hear about the redneck who died and left his wife a trust fund?

She couldn't touch the money till she was fourteen.

• • •

How do they make Polish sausage?

From retarded pigs.

• • •

How many Polacks does it take to have a shower?

Six—one to lie in the bathtub and five to piss on him.

• • •

What's the difference between taxes and a Jewish American Princess?

Taxes suck.

• • •

Why did the Polish woman have an abortion?

She couldn't be sure the baby was hers.

• • •

What do you call a Chinese JAP?

An Orienta.

• • •

Gross Ethnic Jokes

What's the difference between Ted Kennedy and the Polish Army?

Ted Kennedy has at least one confirmed kill.

• • •

What do you call six Italian women in a hot tub?

Gorillas in the mist.

• • •

What do you call an Arab with a goat under one arm and a sheep under the other?

Bisexual.

• • •

How does a Greek firing squad line up?

One behind the other.

• • •

What was the name of the guy who was half Polish and half Chinese?

Sum Dum Fuk.

• • •

What was the name of the Chinese shoe salesman?

Wing Tip Shoo.

• • •

Why are Italians like laxatives?

They irritate the shit out of you.

• • •

Two Polacks were having a drink at the bar. The first Polack says, "You know, it's a dog-eat-dog world out there."

The other Polack replies, "True, but things could be worse. It could be the other way around."

• • •

Hear about the Polish robber who held up a lawyer?

The Polack lost $100.

• • •

How can you tell if a burglar is Polish?

He knocks first.

• • •

Why did the Polack sell his computer?

It didn't get HBO.

• • •

Why did the Polish hemophiliac die?

He went to an acupuncturist.

• • •

Gross Ethnic Jokes

Why are Jewish mothers like parole officers?

They never let anyone finish a sentence.

• • •

The Jewish mother answers the phone. "Hello?" she says.

The voice on the other end of the line says, "I want to rip your clothes off, tie you to the bed, and have sex with you ten different ways, then do it all over again?"

The Jewish mother replies, "All this you know from just saying hello?"

• • •

Hear about the Polish sky diver?

He jumped out of a plane and missed.

• • •

What's a Polish optimist?

A guy who thinks his wife finally gave up cigarettes when he finds cigar butts all around the house.

• • •

What's a black woman's mating call?

"Next!"

• • •

A Polish guy goes to the doctor to see about his constipation. The doctor examines him and says, "What you need to drink is lots of prune juice right after a hot bath."

A week later, the Polack comes back. He's still constipated. The doctor says to him, "So how is the prune juice working?"

The Polack replies, "I don't know. I haven't finished drinking the hot bath yet."

• • •

A black guy goes to the ticket window at the Greyhound bus station. He says to the clerk, "Gimme a round-trip ticket."

The ticket clerk, who is white, asks him, "Where to?"

"Ain't that just like a white man, always wantin' to know the black man's business," the black guy says. "It ain't none of your business where I'm going. Just gimme that ticket!"

• • •

How can you tell the bride at a Polish wedding?

She's the one with the braided armpits.

• • •

What do they call cocaine in Harlem?

Baby powder.

• • •

Gross Ethnic Jokes

Why did Rosa Parks really refuse to move to the back of the bus?

She was just too damn lazy.

• • •

Why did the Texas rancher get angry at his wife?

She couldn't keep her calves together.

• • •

Why do pigeons fly upside down over Italy?

There's nothing worth shitting on.

• • •

Why did the Polack collect burned-out lightbulbs?

He was building a darkroom.

• • •

What's the Polish definition of a washer/dryer?

A douche bag and a towel.

• • •

Hear about the Polish daredevil?

He jumped over twenty motorcycles in a school bus.

• • •

What do you call an Italian who chases garbage trucks?

The galloping gourmet.

• • •

Why are there no zoos in Poland?

The government didn't have enough money to build a fence around it.

• • •

How did the Polack get his head cut off?

He tried feeding breadcrumbs to a helicopter.

• • •

So the warden says to the black inmate, "I'm very sorry, Mr. Jones, but we had a foul-up with your paperwork. We've kept you in prison a month longer than we were supposed to."

The black guy responds, "No problem, Warden. Just take it off my next visit."

• • •

What's the first thing a black kid hears on his tenth birthday?

"Freeze, motherfucker!"

• • •

Gross Ethnic Jokes

How does a Jewish American Princess do it doggie-style?

She rolls over and plays dead.

• • •

Why are there no Polish monks?

The vow of silence includes farting.

• • •

Why did the schools stop teaching sex education in Poland?

The sheep couldn't handle it.

• • •

What do you get when you cross a black man and a goat?

A lawnmower that doesn't work.

• • •

Why do Polish women have breast enlargements?

So they don't have to pay a flat tax.

• • •

The Polish farmer says to his neighbor, who is carrying a burlap bag over his shoulder, "Hey, Stan, if I guess how many chickens you got in that bag, can I have one?"

His neighbor says, "I don't need them. You can have them both."

The Polack says, "All right. There's five."

• • •

How come there are no black workers at Microsoft?

They won't do WINDOWS.

• • •

Carmine the bookie passes away suddenly. All of his Italian friends and customers from his Brooklyn neighborhood show for the funeral.

The priest steps up to the pulpit to deliver the eulogy. "Remember this," he says, "Carmine isn't dead, he's sleeping in that sweet land of Eternity."

"I seen Carmine's body," comes a rough voice from the back of the chapel. "A hundred bucks says he's dead."

• • •

What's Tupac spelled backwards?

Caput.

• • •

What do you call a rapper who dies in a drive-by shooting?

A rap hit everyone can enjoy.

Gross Ethnic Jokes

How did the FBI break up the Million Man March?

They dropped job applications from helicopters.

• • •

How do you know when a Polack has robbed your house?

The dog is pregnant and the garbage cans are empty.

• • •

Why do black people always kill each other?

Who cares?

• • •

What's the worst thing you can say to a Mexican?

"Be yourself."

• • •

What's the difference between a rich Jew and a poor Jew?

A poor Jew has to wash his own Mercedes.

• • •

Why aren't there any dogs in the Vatican?

They like to piss on Poles.

• • •

So Epstein, after three very hard years, graduates from law school with honors. Since he's never been laid in his twenty-four years, he decides to spend all his money going to a whorehouse. Trouble is, he's only got nine dollars. He goes to the whorehouse anyway.

The madam says to him, "I've got this gorgeous blonde, just flew in from Stockholm. She's yours for fifty dollars."

Epstein says, "I'm sorry, but I couldn't afford that."

The madam says, "No problem. I've also got a nice Polish girl. Only thirty dollars."

Epstein says, "I'm sorry, but I can't afford her."

"Okay, how about a black gal for ten dollars."

Epstein tells the madam, "I'm sorry. I've only got nine dollars."

The madam thinks about it for a minute, then says, "All right. Nine dollars is nine dollars. I'll take you on myself."

Epstein has sex with the madam and goes away happy.

Eighteen years go by. Epstein is now a successful lawyer, worth a few million, and has a beautiful wife and family. Life is good. Then, one afternoon, the old madam shows up at his office, with a teenage boy in tow.

The madam says to Epstein, "Do you remember me?"

Epstein says, "No, I don't think I do."

The madam says, "Eighteen years ago, you came to my whorehouse. You only had nine dollars, so I took you on myself." She points to the teenage boy. "This is your son."

Epstein is nobody's fool.

He writes out a check for $30,000 and signs it "Alvin Epstein." He hands it to the boy.

"Alvin Epstein?" he says. "You mean I'm a lousy Jew?"

"Don't complain, kid. Another buck and you'd have been a nigger."

• • •

What's the Italian definition of "bigamist"?

A very dense fog bank.

• • •

A monkey and a black man are sitting in a tree. What do you call the black man?

The assistant branch manager.

• • •

How many pieces does a Polish jigsaw puzzle have?

One.

• • •

The Jew says to the genealogist, "How much would it cost to trace my family tree back to the old country?"

"Five thousand dollars," she tells him.

"Too much," the Jew says. "Is there any way to do it cheaper?"

"Yeah," she says. "Try running for President."

• • •

A Polack comes to New York City on vacation. He goes into a fancy bar-restaurant and runs up a bill of one hundred dollars.

"This is outrageous," the Polack complains. "Back in Poland, you can drink as much as you want without paying. You can sleep in the finest hotels for free, and when you wake up in the morning, there's fifty dollars on the pillow next to you."

"Give me a break," the bartender says. "Has that ever actually happened to you?"

"No, not really," the Polack says. "But my wife says it happens all the time."

• • •

Why did the black farmer try to breed an octopus with a chicken?

So everyone in the family could have a leg.

• • •

What did the sign at the movie theater in Alabama say?

"CHILDREN UNDER THIRTEEN NOT ADMITTED UNLESS ACCOMPANIED BY THEIR HUSBANDS."

The Polack comes home from work one night and is stopped by his neighbor, who tells him, "It may be none of my business, but this afternoon a strange man came to your house and your wife let him in. I peeked through the blinds and I saw them making passionate love."

The Polack asks, "Was he tall, about six feet?"

The neighbor answers, "Yes, I think he was."

"Did he wear glasses and have red hair?" the Polack asks.

"Yes," the neighbor agrees.

"Then that was just the mailman," the Polack responds. "He'll fuck anyone!"

• • •

How do you know when you're truly living in Alabama?

You get married for the third time and you still have the same in-laws.

• • •

How do you know you're really living in Alabama?

You have a home that's mobile and ten cars in the front yard that aren't.

• • •

How do you know when you're at a Polish wedding?

The groom is wearing a clean bowling shirt.

• • •

What are a Jewish baby's first words?

"Trust fund."

• • •

Five Italians are playing poker, as they do every Friday. At midnight, Louie comes back from the bathroom and says to their host, "Hey, Nick, I just seen Guido makin' love to your wife in the kitchen."

"Okay, that's it, guys," Nick says. "This is positively the last deal."

• • •

Why did the Polish butcher fall behind in his work?

He backed into the meat grinder.

• • •

What's a Puerto Rican vacation?

Hanging out on the neighbor's stoop with a six-pack.

• • •

After the wedding, Marie is taken upstairs by the groom, Tony. Five minutes later, Marie comes running downstairs into the kitchen, where her mother is making tea.

"Mama," Marie exclaims. "Tony, he's gotta hair all over his chest."

"He's-a supposed to have hair on his chest," Mama says. "You go back-a upstairs."

Five minutes later, Marie comes charging back into the kitchen.

"Mama, Mama," Marie cries. "Tony, he's-a gotta hair on his legs."

"He's-a supposed to have the hair on the legs," Mama says. "You go back-a upstairs."

There, Tony takes off his shoes and socks, revealing a clubfoot.

Marie runs back into the kitchen and declares, "Tony, he's only a halfa foot."

Mama's eyes light up. She says to her daughter, "You stay-a here. I'm-a going upstairs."

* * *

What do you call it when a Jew farts in a blizzard?

A kosher cold cut.

5

GROSS CELEBRITY JOKES

● ● ● ● ● ●

What do you call Roseanne holding a million dollars?

A cash cow.

• • •

What does O.J. Simpson have in common with Michael Jackson?

They both missed a glove and both were under the knife.

• • •

What's the name of Roseanne's new sitcom?

three-thirty-something.

• • •

What did Susan Smith's employer do when he found out she drowned her two children?

He docked her pay.

• • •

Did you hear that Marlee Martin and Helen Keller are doing comedy together?

It's called "Def Comedy Jam."

What happened when Ted Kennedy couldn't find his glasses?

He drank straight from the bottle.

• • •

What did Madonna do when she turned frigid?

She fucked her psychiatrist.

• • •

Why was Ted Bundy a bad golfer?

He always took a few slices before he put it in the hole.

• • •

How do you know when it's bedtime at Michael Jackson's house?

The big hand touches the little hand.

• • •

What do Branch Davidians and Wendy's hamburgers have in common?

They're both well done by Dave.

• • •

What's the difference between O.J. and Colonel Sanders?

Colonel Sanders kills his chicks before he batters them.

• • •

Hear about the new O.J. Simpson perfume?

You just slap it on.

• • •

What's the Spanish word for Rodney King?

Piñata.

• • •

Hear about the new Rodney King poker game?

Four clubs beat one spade.

• • •

Why does Bill Clinton have a clear conscience?

He's never used it.

• • •

What can Mark Fuhrman do that a black woman can't?

Get O.J. off.

• • •

How does Snow White get seven inches of cock?

One inch at a time.

• • •

What do you get when you cross a convertible and Madonna?

A singer whose top comes right off.

• • •

Why are Michael Jackson's pants so short?

Because they're not his.

• • •

Why did Michael Jackson give up Pepsi?

He switched to Seven & Up.

• • •

Why did Kato Kaelin wear tennis shoes to the O.J. trial?

He heard there was going to be recess.

• • •

What's the difference between John and Lorena Bobbitt?

She's crazy and he's just nuts.

• • •

What did Bill Clinton tell Hillary after sex?

"I'll be home in twenty minutes."

• • •

So Newt Gingrich, Bob Dole, and Bill Clinton find themselves in the land of Oz. They follow the Yellow Brick Road and meet the Wizard, who grants each of them one request.

Gingrich asks for a brain. He gets one.

Dole asks for a heart. He gets one.

Clinton asks the Wizard, "Is that Dorothy still around?"

• • •

What did Woody Allen say to Michael Jackson?

"I'll give you two tens for a twenty."

• • •

What's the definition of saturated fat?

Rush Limbaugh in a hot tub.

• • •

Bumper sticker of the month: "If Clinton is the answer, it was probably a stupid question."

• • •

What do you get when you cross Dr. Kevorkian, Dr. Ruth, and Tonya Harding?

Drop-dead sex that will bring you to your knees.

• • •

What's the best thing about living next door to a Hare Krishna?

You can always get a free ride to the airport.

• • •

What's the difference between O.J. Simpson and Pee Wee Herman?

It only took ten jerks to get Pee Wee off.

• • •

What do you call a Deadhead who just broke up with his girlfriend?

Homeless.

• • •

Hear about the new Bill Clinton golf ball?

It's guaranteed a perfect lie every time.

• • •

How did Bill Clinton slow down inflation?

He handed it over to the post office.

• • •

Gross Celebrity Jokes

Hear about the new Marilyn Monroe stamp?

When you lick it, you feel just like a Kennedy.

• • •

What did Bob Hope do on Labor Day?

He entertained the troops guarding the White House.

• • •

How do you know when your house has been robbed by a Deadhead?

Your thongs are missing.

• • •

Why did Michael Jackson quit the Cub Scouts?

He was up to a pack a day.

• • •

Hear about the new Heidi Fleiss doll?

When you buy one, she gets you another doll.

• • •

Why did they take John Wayne toilet paper off the market?

It wouldn't take shit from anyone.

• • •

So the very attractive woman spots a man in the elevator with her and he looks familiar.

She says, "Aren't you Donald Trump?"

"As a matter of fact, I am," Trump replies.

"I think you're great," the woman says. "How would you like to go back to my room? I'll give you a blow job you'll never forget, and then I'll fuck you six ways from Sunday."

"I don't know," Trump replies. "What's in it for me?"

• • •

What does "Magic" stand for?

"My Ass Got Infected, Coach."

• • •

What did Ted Kennedy say to Judge Clarence Thomas during the Anita Hill hearings?

"Why didn't you just drown the bitch?"

• • •

What do Magic Johnson and Rock Hudson have in common?

They both got a hold of some bad crack.

• • •

Why did David Copperfield get AIDS?

He was doing Magic.

Gross Celebrity Jokes

Why did Rosie O'Donnell stop going to the beach?

Because the Save the Whales people kept pushing her back into the ocean.

• • •

What do you get when you cross David Duke and Oliver North?

Ku Klux Klan and Ollie.

• • •

What was Jeffrey Dahmer's favorite meal?

Frank and beans.

• • •

What did Jeffrey Dahmer have for his last meal?

Stew.

• • •

Who did cops find in Jeffrey Dahmer's refrigerator?

Oscar Meyer.

• • •

What's the difference between Michael Jackson and Mr. Potatohead?

Michael Jackson has had more noses.

• • •

What's Mr. Potatohead's new movie?
My Own Private Idaho.

• • •

Why was John F. Kennedy such a lousy boxer?
He couldn't take a shot to the head.

• • •

What's Jimmy Swaggart's favorite magazine?
Re-Penthouse.

• • •

What's the definition of endless love?
Stevie Wonder playing tennis with Ray Charles.

• • •

What's the difference between Hillary Clinton and a shark?
Nail polish.

6

GAYS
AND
LESBIANS

● ● ● ● ● ●

What do you get when you cross fifty lesbians and fifty politicians?

A hundred people who don't do dick.

• • •

Bruce came home from work. His lover, Stanley, said to him, "Oh, Brucie, it feels like I've got something stuck in my asshole. Could you take a look?"

Bruce told Stanley to bend over and took a peek up his lover's blowhole. "I don't see anything up there, Stanley."

Stanley replied, "But there is, I can feel it. Stick a finger in there and maybe you'll feel something."

Bruce complied. "I still don't feel anything, Stanley."

Stanley said, "I know something's up there, I can feel it. Stick another finger up there."

Bruce did, sticking two fingers up Stanley's poop-chute. Bruce said, "I still don't feel anything."

Stanley said, "Try putting your hand up there."

Bruce shoved his hand way up Stanley's asshole. When he pulled it out, there was a thousand-dollar Rolex watch on his wrist.

Bruce said, amazed, "What the hell—"

Stanley said, "Happy birthday to you, happy birthday to you . . ."

What kind of bread do faggots like best?

Humper-nickel.

• • •

Little Johnny came home from school, crying his eyes out. His mother said, "Johnny, why are you crying?"

Johnny replied, "Because Stevie called me a sissy!"

"What did you do?" his mother asked.

"I hit him with my purse!"

• • •

What do you call a gay fruit?

A fig-git.

• • •

A rabbi and a priest accidentally walk into a gay bar. They are barely seated when a young man walks over to the priest and asks him for the next dance.

Horrified, the priest turns to the rabbi and says, "Please help me out of this, Sidney."

The rabbi whispers something into the faggot's ear, and he walks away. The priest, visibly relieved, asks the rabbi, "What did you say to him, Sid?"

The rabbi replies, "I told him we were on our honeymoon."

• • •

Gays and Lesbians

A fag walks into a sex shop and starts looking over the rubber dildoes. He sees one he really likes: a twelve-inch black one. Pointing to the huge rubber dick, he says to the clerk, "I'll take that one."

The clerk says, "Should I wrap it up?"

The fag replies, "No thanks, I'll eat it here."

• • •

What do you call a gay masochist?

A sucker for punishment.

• • •

A gay man goes to see his doctor, who tells him, "The news is bad, very bad. I'm afraid you've tested positive. You've got AIDS."

"That's terrible," the gay guy says. "What should I do?"

The doctor says, "Go to Mexico."

"Mexico?" the gay guy asks.

"That's right," the doctor says. "Drink the water, eat lots of Mexican food, especially the raw fruit and vegetables."

"Will that cure my AIDS?"

"No, but it will definitely teach you what your asshole is for."

• • •

What's the definition of confusion?

Twenty blind lesbians in a fish market.

So Joel and Evan are walking along the beach when they spot a bottle half-buried in the sand. Upon rubbing it a genie pops out.

The genie looks them over and says, "Are you two guys gay?"

Joel and Evan admit that they are, so the genie says, "To speak the plain truth, I don't like gay people. But you've freed me from this bottle after thousands of years, so I'm supposed to grant you three wishes. Instead, I'll grant you one wish. Think carefully, and when you're ready, just make the wish."

The genie disappears. Joel and Evan return to their hotel room.

A few minutes later, the door burst open and a dozen white-sheeted men storm into the place.

"We're the KKK," one of them says, "and we're gonna string you-all up!"

Sure enough, the klansmen start putting ropes around the faggots' necks.

"Joel," Evan says to his lover, "this might be a good time to make that wish."

Evan replies, "I already did."

"What do you mean, you already did?" Joel asks as he feels the rope tighten around his neck.

"I wished that we could both be hung like niggers," Evan says.

• • •

What is the AIDS hotline number?

1-800-TOO-LATE.

Gays and Lesbians

What do lawyers and male prostitutes have in common?

They both make their living fucking people up the ass.

• • •

What do lesbians give their lovers on Christmas?

Gift-wrapped batteries.

• • •

What's the most popular comic book in Greenwich Village?

Teenage Mutant Ninja Gerbils.

• • •

What's the difference between AIDS and golf?

In golf one bad hole won't kill you.

• • •

What's the difference between a fag and a refrigerator?

A refrigerator doesn't fart when you pull the meat out.

• • •

How do you know when you're in a dyke bar?

Even the pool table doesn't have any balls.

How may fags does it take to mug an old lady?

Five—four to hold her down and one to do her hair.

• • •

What is 71?

69 with two fingers up your ass.

• • •

How did the young guy know he was bisexual?

He was only half in Earnest.

• • •

What happened to the gay Eskimos?

They good Kool-AIDS.

• • •

How do faggots play Russian Roulette?

They pass around six boys, and one of them has AIDS.

• • •

How does a fag know when spring has arrived?

A gerbil comes out of his ass and doesn't see its shadow.

• • •

What present did the fag hairdresser want for his birthday?

To be teased and blown.

• • •

Hear about the gay midget?

He came out of the cupboard.

• • •

What's the definition of an anal suppository?

A chastity belt for fags.

• • •

What's the definition of GAY?

Got AIDS Yet?

• • •

What's the difference between a fag and a suppository?

About four inches.

• • •

Why were gay men the first ones to leave town when the earthquake struck?

They already had their shit packed.

• • •

What do a male hustler and a lawyer have in common?

They both make their living fucking people up the ass.

• • •

Why did the San Francisco Police Department fire the gay detectives?

Because they blew all their cases.

• • •

Why do fags act like such pricks?

You are what you eat.

• • •

Why did the fag get fired from the Hershey plant?

He didn't pack enough fudge.

• • •

What's the definition of an open can of sardines?

Lesbian potpourri.

• • •

Gays and Lesbians

Hear about the gay burglar?

He couldn't blow the safe, so he went down on the elevator.

• • •

What do you call two lesbians in a canoe?

Fur traders.

• • •

Hear about the JAP who was bisexual?

Twice a year was too much.

• • •

Hear about the gay termite?

He went for the woodpecker.

• • •

Why did the gay golfer go to Puerto Rico?

He wanted a hole in Juan.

• • •

Hear about the gay Canadian Mountie?

He not only gets his man, he gets to keep him.

• • •

So this gay couple get into a fight and break up. As Bruce is packing, he says to Stanley, "And I'm taking all the Streisand CDs with me."

"Well, you know what you can do with them!" Stanley says.

"Don't you dare try making up with me."

• • •

Why do gay men grow mustaches?

To hide their stretch marks.

• • •

Why did the fag get fired from his job at the sperm bank?

He was caught drinking on the job.

• • •

Hear about the queer Dutch boy who stuck his finger in a dyke?

She beat the crap out of him.

• • •

What's the difference between lesbian and whales?

No one is trying to save the lesbians.

• • •

What's a fag's favorite dish at a Chinese restaurant?

Sum yung guy.

Gays and Lesbians

Why did the Jewish lesbian move to Israel?
She missed the Hebrew tongue.

• • •

Hear about the transvestites who got arrested?
They were booked for male fraud.

• • •

Then there was the guy who gave his first blow job.
He woke up with a queer taste in his mouth.

• • •

So the Jewish fag says to his roommate, "Sidney, did the rabbi come yet?"
    "No," the roomie says, "but he's starting to moan."

• • •

Hear about the gay Polack?
He liked women.

• • •

Why did the gay security guard get fired?
He was bending over on the job.

• • •

What did the lesbian bumper sticker say?
"Save a tree. Eat a beaver."

What's a lesbian's favorite pet?

A lap dog.

• • •

Hear about the popsicle for queers?

It's got hair around the stick.

7

NOW
THAT'S
SICK!

● ● ● ● ● ● ●

What's the difference between two beers and a piss?

About twenty minutes.

• • •

What happened to the cannibal who ate a rabbi and a priest?

He had a religious movement.

• • •

So Murray and his wife retire for the night. Edna goes right to sleep, but Murray decides to stay up and read for a while. Every few minutes, Murray tickles his wife's pussy, then continues reading.

Finally, Edna says, "Murray, would you please stop teasing me like that."

Murray responds, "I'm not teasing you, Edna. I'm wetting my finger so I can turn the page."

• • •

What's the difference between sex for money and sex for free?

Sex for free costs a hell of a lot more.

• • •

So Sam says to the psychiatrist, "Doc, I work in a pickle factory, and I have this uncontrollable urge to stick my dick into the pickle slicer. What should I do?"

The shrink thinks for a moment and says, "I had a patient last year who had a similar urge to put his hand on a hot stove."

"What happened?" Sam asks.

"I told him to go ahead and do it," the shrink replies, "and it cured him forever. My advice to you is, go ahead and give in to your urge."

A week later, Sam came back and said to the shrink. "Well, I took your advice and stuck my dick into the pickle slicer."

"And what happened?"

"She and I both got fired."

• • •

What do you call a mountain climber who just had a vasectomy?

Dry sack on the rocks.

• • •

On the fourth day of their honeymoon—after Phil and his new bride had been screwing nonstop—they decided to catch some rays on the nude beach. Phil got his cock sunburned so badly, he found it too painful to have sex. He went to a local doctor, who told him, "Stick your cock in a glass of cold milk."

That evening, he did just that. His bride came in and saw what he was doing. She said, "Aha! Now I know how you guys reload that thing!"

Now That's Sick!

What do you call a prostitute who works at an inter-state exit?

A tollhouse cookie.

• • •

How long does it take for a woman to achieve orgasm?

Who the hell cares?

• • •

What's cold but still smokes like a chimney?

A blonde.

• • •

Fourteen-year-old Willie came home and told his mother that he'd just gotten laid for the first time. His mother was shocked and slapped him. She said, "Go to your room and just wait until your father gets home."

Willie went upstairs to his room. An hour later, his father opened the door, grinning from ear to ear. "So," he said, "your mother tells me you got laid today for the first time. I'm proud of you, son. How did it feel?"

"It felt okay, but next time I'm using Vaseline. My asshole hurts like hell!"

• • •

How many male chauvinists does it take to screw in a lightbulb?

None—let the bitch do it.

• • •

What do you get when you cross a pit bull with a St. Bernard?

A dog that rips you to pieces, then gives you a drink of whiskey.

• • •

The nymphomaniac said to her friend. "I have this strange problem. Every time I sneeze, I have an incredible orgasm."

Her friend asks, "What are you doing about it?"

"I'm taking snuff."

• • •

What did the sadist give the blind man for Christmas?

A paint-by-number set.

• • •

What do you call the white stuff found in a blonde's panties?

Clitty litter.

• • •

Now That's Sick!

What do fat women and mopeds have in common?

They're both fun to ride until your friends see you.

• • •

What did the blonde do when the doctor told her she had sugar in her urine?

She pissed in her cornflakes.

• • •

Hear about the woman whose boyfriend said he loved her?

She believed him.

• • •

How do you brainwash an Italian woman?

Step on her douche bag.

• • •

What's the definition of an overbite?

Eating pussy and tasting shit.

• • •

Bill discovers shortly after getting married that his wife is a total nymphomaniac, who'll have sex with any man who asks her. Alarmed, he takes her to the doctor for an exam.

Bill says to the doctor, "My wife will fuck anyone, and it makes me very jealous. Is there anything you can do?"

The doctor agrees to examine her. He takes Bill's wife into the examination room, then tells her to undress and lie on her stomach on the table. He starts feeling her ass cheeks and her twat. She starts to squirm and moan. The doctor gets so horny, he rips off his clothes, jumps on top of her, and starts screwing her brains out.

Bill barges into the room and sees the doctor, stark naked, humping his wife. Bill says, "Just what the hell do you think you're doing?"

The doctor stammers, "I'm, uh, taking your wife's temperature."

Bill takes out a gun and puts the barrel to the doctor's head. Bill says, "When you take that thing out, Doc, it better have red numbers on it!"

• • •

The gynecologist finishes examining the woman and tells her, "I'm sorry, Mrs. Jones, but removing the vibrator from your vagina is going to be a very delicate and expensive procedure."

"I'm not sure I can afford it," his patient replies. "Why don't you just replace the batteries?"

• • •

Now That's Sick!

Hear about the hooker who scheduled two appointments for the same time?

She managed to squeeze them both in.

• • •

Why do Polish babies have such big heads?

So they don't fall out during the wedding polka dance.

• • •

What's the difference between a porcupine and three lawyers in a BMW?

A porcupine has its pricks on the outside.

• • •

How did the husband know his wife was fucking their German shepherd?

He caught her douching with Gravy Train.

• • •

"Mommy, Mommy! Can't we give Daddy a decent burial?"

"Shut up and keep flushing!"

• • •

The wife calls her husband at the office and says, near panic, "Little Billy just ate a box of rat poison!"

"Don't worry, dear," hubby says. "He'll just crawl under the house to die."

• • •

What was the most popular item at the Polish-Cajun restaurant?

Blackened toast.

• • •

How did the blonde pierce her ear?

She answered the stapler.

• • •

What's the difference between an ugly girl and a pretty girl?

Nine beers.

• • •

Why did God invent liquor?

So ugly girls could get laid, too.

• • •

What's the definition of a lap dog?

An ugly girl who gives great head.

• • •

Now That's Sick!

Why are single men skinny, and married men fat?

A single guy comes home, sees what's in the refrigerator, and goes to bed. A married guy comes home, sees what's in bed, and goes to the refrigerator.

• • •

Why didn't Jesus Christ get into college?

He got hung up on the boards.

• • •

What did they rename Waco after the Branch Davidian massacre?

Corpus Crispy.

• • •

How do you get fifteen Puerto Ricans out of a car?

Spray in some Lysol.

• • •

This polish guy goes to the airport and says to the ticket agent, "How long does it take to fly to Poland?"

The ticket agent is very busy. He says to the Polack, "Just a minute, sir."

The Polack says, "Thank you," and leaves.

• • •

This young female intern is working at a nursing home. She meets Mrs. Schwartz, who is ninety-nine years old. The intern starts examining Mrs. Schwartz, who asks the pretty young doctor, "Are you married, sweetheart?"

"Yes," the female intern replies. "My husband and I have been married for a year."

Mrs. Schwartz asks her, "Any children yet?"

"My husband is a stockbroker and I'm hoping to become a doctor. We just don't have the time to have children."

"Time, shmime," Mrs. Schwartz snorts. "My husband and I had six children. We have sixteen grandchildren, ten great-grandchildren, and the whole thing took only fifteen minutes!"

• • •

"So how's your husband?" Annie's mother asks her daughter.

"Not so good, Mom," Annie says. "He cut his finger on a bread knife and he's in the hospital for two weeks."

"That seems like a long time for a simple cut," Annie's mother says. "Have you seen the doctor?"

"No," Annie replies. "But I've seen the nurse."

• • •

Why did God create businessmen?

To make weathermen look good.

• • •

Now That's Sick!

So the candidate for governor says to his constituents, "I promise to lower taxes, reduce illegal immigration, and clean up dirty politics."

A man in the crowd says, "You're a lying sack of shit!"

"Yes, I am," the politician says. "Just let me finish."

• • •

A man goes to his doctor because he's having trouble breathing. The doctor takes a look up the man's nose and gasps.

The doctor says to the patient, "Did you know you have cauliflower growing in your nose?"

"That's terrible, doc," the patient says. "I planted marijuana!"

• • •

What's the difference between Johnny Cochran and Divine Brown?

At least Johnny Cochran got his client off.

• • •

What's the difference between a money launderer and a congressman?

Once in a while, a money launderer passes a few good bills.

• • •

What did the loser do before the cockfight?

He greased his zipper.

• • •

What's the definition of wicker box?

What Elmer Fudd wants to do to Madonna.

• • •

What's the definition of a hysterectomy?

When you remove the nursery but leave the playpen.

• • •

What did the first psychiatrist say to the second psychiatrist when they met on the street?

"You're fine. How am I?"

• • •

What do you get when you cross a rooster and a chick who works for AT&T?

A cock that wants to reach out and touch someone.

• • •

Now That's Sick!

Hear about the Polack who couldn't spell?

He spent the night in a warehouse.

• • •

Where do masochists have lunch?

At a snack bar.

• • •

Why did the Japanese leper commit suicide?

Because he lost face.

• • •

What's green and has an IQ of 160?

A platoon of marines.

• • •

What's the definition of real pain?

Jumping off the Empire State Building and catching your eyelid on a nail.

• • •

Tom can't decide which of his three girlfriends he wants to marry, so he gives them a test. He gives them each five thousand dollars and tells them to spend it any way they want.

The first girlfriend spends it on a new wardrobe and tells him, "I wanted to look really nice so you'd want to marry me."

The second girlfriend takes the five thousand and refurnishes Tom's apartment. She says, "I wanted you to have a nice place for when we get married."

The third girlfriend invests her five thousand on Wall Street and turns it into $50,000. She says, "I wanted to make money for us so we could have a great honeymoon and buy a house."

Which girlfriend did the guy marry?

The one with the biggest tits.

• • •

So this couple goes out on a blind date and halfway through dinner the guy decides he can't take another minute. He excuses himself to go to the bathroom, then seeks out his waiter and says, "Call me to the telephone when I get back to the table."

The waiter does and the guy excuses himself and goes to the phone. He comes back to the table and says to his date, "I'm sorry, but I've got to leave. My grandmother just died."

"Thank God," his date says. "If yours hadn't, mine was about to."

• • •

Mrs. O'Brien goes to see the family doctor. She asks him for a remedy to give her husband more sexual stamina.

The doctor hands Mrs. O'Brien a bottle of pills and tells her, "Give your husband one of these each evening and give him a shot of whiskey, too."

A few weeks later, Mrs. O'Brien goes back to see the doctor, who asks her how things are working out.

"Well," she says, "My husband is behind on the pills, but he's six months ahead on the whiskey."

• • •

What's the definition of a lesbian?

A woman trying to do a man's job.

• • •

What do you get when you breed a cat and a rabbit?

A pussy hare.

• • •

What's the definition of love?

The myth that one cunt is different from another cunt.

• • •

What's the name of the airline for senior citizens?

Incontinental.

What's another name for Harlem?

"Scene of the crime."

• • •

What's the definition of conceit?

A flea with a hard-on who asks, "Had enough yet, bitch?"

• • •

Hear about the guy who dropped his wallet in San Francisco?

He had to kick it all the way to Los Angeles before he could pick it up.

• • •

What do you call a guy who's brain-dead, has no arms and legs, and has a twelve-inch cock?

Partially disabled.

• • •

How do you get twenty Mexicans into a phone booth?

Tell them they own it.

• • •

Now That's Sick!

So Harry is two hours late for work. His boss says, "This is the last straw, Harry. You come in late again without a good excuse, your ass is fired."

Two days later, Harry comes in four hours late. The boss says, "Okay, Harry, I said I'd fire you again if you didn't have a good excuse, so it better be good."

"Oh, it's good," Harry replies. "See, I was walking to work, right along the railroad tracks like I always do. And what do I see tied to the tracks but the sexiest damn woman I've ever laid eyes on. Well, I untied her and banged the shit out of her all morning."

"Yeah?" the boss asks. "Did she give you any head?"

"Nah," Harry says. "I couldn't find it.

• • •

How many surrealists does it take to screw in a lightbulb?

Fish.

• • •

What's the recipe for chicken à la Vietnam?

First, napalm a chicken coop, then . . .

• • •

What's the difference between Maine and New Hampshire?

In New Hampshire, Moosehead is a beer. In Maine, it's sexual assault.

So an Italian walks into a bar and orders a martini. He looks down at the end of the bar and sees a guy who looks very familiar.

"Hey," the Italian says, "ain't that Jesus Christ over there?"

"As a matter of fact, it is Jesus Christ," the bartender says.

"I'd like to buy Him a drink," says the Italian.

The bartender gives Jesus Christ a martini. Jesus acknowledges it with a nod and a smile.

A few minutes later, a Polack walks into the bar and orders a beer and a shot. He says to the bartender, "That looks like Jesus Christ!"

"It is Jesus Christ," says the bartender.

The Polack likewise buys Jesus Christ a drink. Jesus acknowledges it with a nod and a smile.

A few minutes later, a black guy comes into the bar and orders a bourbon and soda. He says to the bartender, "Man, is that Jesus Christ?"

"Yes, it is," the bartender says.

The black guy buys Jesus Christ a drink. Jesus acknowledges it with a nod and a smile.

Ten minutes later, Jesus gets up to leave. On the way out, he puts his hand on the Italian's shoulder and says, "Thank you for the drink, my son."

"It's a miracle!" the Italian says. "I had arthritis and was in pain all the time, but your hand has healed me completely!"

Jesus then walks up to the Polack, puts his hand on his shoulder, and thanks him.

The Polack exclaims, "I had a pinched nerve in my back and was in pain all the time, but now I'm healed!"

Jesus walks over to the black guy.

"Yo, man, don't be touching me," the black guy says. "I'm on disability."

• • •

Two Polish terrorists are driving through the streets of Krakow on their way to blow up an embassy. "Hey, Stosh," the first Polack asks, "what happens if that bomb we got in the backseat blows up before we get there?"

"Don't worry," the second Polack replies. "I've got another one in the trunk."

• • •

Why don't Italians barbecue?

The spaghetti keeps falling through the grill.

• • •

How do you know when you live in a really bad neighborhood?

The church has a bouncer.

• • •

How do you know when you're in a Harlem high school?

The school newspaper has an obituary page.

• • •

So the young yuppie husband and wife both get downsized and are flat broke. The only way to make money, the husband decides, is for his wife to work the streets.

So the first night, a car stops on the wife's corner. The john asks her, "How much for straight sex?"

"Just a minute," the wife says, and runs over to where her husband is waiting. "How much should I charge for straight sex?" she asks him.

"Tell him a hundred bucks," the husband says.

She runs back to the waiting john and says, "One hundred bucks."

The john says, "I don't have a hundred. How much for a hand job?"

She runs back to her husband and asks him how much she should charge for a hand job. "Forty bucks," he tells her.

The john agrees to her price and proceeds to pull out a twelve-inch cock.

"Wait a minute," she tells the john, and rushes back to her husband. "Honey," she asks, "can we lend that nice man sixty dollars?"

• • •

Now That's Sick!

So the Jewish guy comes home early from work one day. As he pulls up, he sees a plumber's truck in the driveway.

"Please Lord," the husband prays, "let her be having an affair!"

• • •

What did Jesus say to Mary when he was on the cross?

"Can you get me my flats? These spikes are killing me."

• • •

What did one unemployed yuppie say to the other?

"There's no such thing as a free brunch."

• • •

So the racist loses his job as a furniture salesman and joins the police force. His first week on the job, he kills a dozen drug dealers, bank robbers, and other assorted criminals, all of them black.

"So, how's the job coming?" the new cop's best friend asks one day.

"Just great," the racist says. "What I like best about it is, the customer is always wrong."

• • •

How do you know Jesus Christ wasn't really born in Italy?

Three wise men and a virgin? Come on.

• • •

What are the three best things about women?

They bleed without cutting themselves.
They can bury a bone without digging a hole.
They can make a man come without calling.

• • •

Jake and Sam are sitting on a park bench. Sam says, "So Jake, how's the wife?"

"To tell you the truth," Jake replies, "I think she's dead."

Sam is shocked. He says, "How can you say such a thing? What do you mean she's dead?"

"Well," Jake says, "The sex is the same, but the dirty dishes are piling up in the sink."

• • •

What do you call making love to a porcupine?

Prickly heat.

• • •

What do you call a midget circumcision?

A Tiny Trim.

• • •

What's the definition of eternity?

The hour between when you come and she leaves.

• • •

How do you know when you're really getting old?

You're with a woman all night long and the only thing that comes is the dawn.

• • •

Why is it bad when a blond has PMS?

It stands for Permanent Mental State.

• • •

What's the difference between an in-law and an outlaw?

An outlaw doesn't want to live in your guest room.

• • •

What's the definition of pile carpeting?

Hair on hemorrhoids.

• • •

What's the best way to find a whore who gives golden showers?

Follow the yellow brick road.

• • •

What's the definition of gross?

Getting a hard-on and running out of skin.

• • •

What's the difference between men and women?

Women play hard to get; men get hard to play.

• • •

Why did the girl leave the convent?

She found out that *nun* really means *none*.

• • •

When is it time to stop screwing doggie style?

When your girlfriend starts chasing cars.

• • •

So one woman boasts to her best friend, "I have two boyfriends, and I've never been happier. One is handsome, kind, caring, and considerate."

"Then what do you need a second one for?"
"Because he's straight."

• • •

How many Hollywood agents does it take to screw in a lightbulb?

Ten—but they'll accept eight.

• • •

Now That's Sick!

So the guy goes to his doctor. The guy's cock is covered with green and purple spots.

"My God," the doctor exclaims. "How did that happen?"

"I don't exactly know, doc," the guy says. "I was driving down 42nd Street when I spotted this gorgeous blond hooker. I made love to her all night and then a week later, this." He points to his multicolored cock. "What should I do?"

"Next time take 34th Street."

• • •

What's the definition of an optimist?

An accordion player with a beeper.

• • •

What's another definition of an optimist?

A promiscuous queer who buys an IRA.

• • •

Why do men swim faster than women?

They have a built-in rudder.

• • •

What's the true purpose of toilet paper?

Film for your brownie.

• • •

So the doctor says to the husband, "I think we can cure your sexual dysfunction. But it's very expensive."

"How expensive?" the husband says.

"Well, one procedure is $15,000 and is seventy percent effective. The second procedure is $20,000 and is one hundred percent effective. So here's what I suggest," the doctor continues. "Go home and discuss it with your wife, then come back when you've made your decision."

Two days later, the husband comes back. The doctor asks him, "Which procedure have you decided on?"

"Neither," the husband replies. "We decided to remodel the kitchen instead."

• • •

So Joe and Eddie are having some beers. Something is troubling Eddie, Joe can tell. After a lot of prodding, Eddie finally blurts out, "Okay, the trouble is your wife."

"My wife?" Joe asks. "What about her?"

"I think she's cheating on us."

• • •

Now That's Sick!

How do you get twenty yuppies into a minivan?

Promote one and watch the other nineteen climb up his ass.

• • •

What do you call a lesbian with fat fingers?

Well hung.

• • •

What's a typical WASP ménage à trois?

Two headaches and a hard-on.

• • •

The newlyweds were uncomfortable using the word "sex," so they agreed to refer to their lovemaking as "doing the laundry." This went on for years, even after their children were born.

One day the husband felt in the mood and sent his young son downstairs to ask his wife if she wanted to do the laundry. Fifteen minutes passed, then a half hour, then an hour and a half. Finally the kid came back and told his father, "Mommy says she'll do the laundry in five minutes."

"Tell her not to bother," the father said. "Tell her it was a small load and I did it myself."

• • •

"The man next to me is jerking off!" cries the girl to her friend in the dark movie house.

"Just ignore him," her friend says.

"I can't. He's using my hand."

• • •

What happens when a girl puts her panties on backwards?

She gets her ass chewed out.

• • •

What are brownie points?

Things you find in a Brownie's bra.

• • •

What's oral sex in Chinese?

Tung chow.

• • •

What's oral sex with an unhygienic Chinese girl?

Tung chow yuk.

• • •

Now That's Sick!

What's a Chinese guy with constipation?

Hung dung.

• • •

So Phil goes to the barbershop for a haircut. The barber points to a curly blond hair in Phil's mustache. "Where'd that come from?"

Phil says, "Oh that? Every morning before I leave, I give my wife a kiss on the head."

"Okay," the barber says. "Thing is, you've got shit all over your necktie."

• • •

What's the difference between a pussy and a cunt?

A pussy is soft and warm and inviting . . . and a cunt is the one who owns it.

• • •

What do you call a blond between two brunets?

A mental block.

• • •

Why are Italian hookers so busy?

They never let a dago by.

• • •

What's the definition of a moron?

A guy who thinks his wife is going to church when she comes home with a Gideon Bible.

• • •

What would Joey Buttafucco be if he went to Harvard?

A Kennedy.

• • •

Hear about the priest who gave up drinking?

It was the longest ten minutes of his life.

• • •

What do you call a German with a hard-on?

A frau-loader.

• • •

What's the definition of artificial insemination?

A technical knock-up.

• • •

So Murray is romping in bed with a married woman when they hear the garage door open.

"It's my husband," the frantic woman cries. "Get out of bed and start ironing these." She tosses a bunch of shirts at him.

The husband strolls in and asks his wife about the strange man ironing shirts.

"He's our new housekeeper," the wife says.

Her husband seems to accept the explanation. Murray stays and finishes ironing the shirts. Later, he leaves and walks to the corner to catch the bus. He can't help but start bragging about his narrow escape and relates his experience to a man waiting next to him at the bus stop.

The man says to Murray, "Are you talking about the redhead who lives in the brick house over there?"

"Yes, I am," Murray admits.

"Hell, son," the man says. "I'm the one who *washed* the shirts."

• • •

What's Helen Keller's favorite mouthwash?

Jergen's hand lotion.

• • •

What's the definition of a Jewish "10"?

A girl with two tits and eight million dollars.

• • •

Why do blondes like cars with sunroofs?

There's more leg room.

What happened to the leper when he walked into the screen door?

He strained himself.

• • •

So Goldberg says to Cohen, "My wife and I took a class in efficiency."

"Why did you do that?" Cohen asks.

"Well," Goldberg says, "I noticed my wife's routine at breakfast for years. She made dozens of trips between the stove, refrigerator, and the table, always carrying one dish at a time. So we took this class."

"Did it help?"

"It sure did. It used to take her twenty minutes to put breakfast on the table. Now it only takes me seven."

• • •

What did the flasher say to the woman in Alaska?

"It's really cold. Mind if I just describe myself?"

• • •

What's the definition of henpecked?

A sterile husband who is afraid to tell his pregnant wife.

• • •

The prisoner is escorted by two guards to the conference room at the jail, where his attorney is waiting.

"Sam," the prisoner says, "you gotta get me out of here."

"Jack, don't worry," the lawyer says to his hand-cuffed client. "Everything's cool. Even if I can't prove to the jury that you were out of town on the night of the triple murder, I have two shrinks who'll testify that you were insane. Just in case, I'll pay off all of the district attorney's witnesses. Also, the judge is a good friend and he owes me one, big time."

"That's great," the prisoner says. "What do I need to do?"

The lawyer says, "Just to be safe, try and escape."

• • •

How do you know when your lawyer is well hung?

You can't get your fingers between his neck and the noose.

• • •

What's the difference between McDonald's and a black prostitute?

McDonald's has only served 100 million.

• • •

What do you get when you cross a black man and an ape?

A monkeyshine.

• • •

What do you call a retired black prostitute?

Grandma.

• • •

So a cop in Harlem sees an old black woman kicking a can down the street. He says to her, "What are you doing?"

"I'm moving," she says.

• • •

What happened when the two queers got into an argument?

They exchanged blows.

• • •

What do you call a baby before it's born?

Daddy's little squirt.

• • •

Now That's Sick!

Why is a Jewish divorce so expensive?

Because it's worth it.

• • •

What do you get when you cross Arnold Schwarzenegger and a Jew?

Conan the Wholesaler.

• • •

Hear about the Italian inflatable doll?

Put a ring on her finger and her hips expand.

• • •

How do you know when a Jew is really cheap?

He can't even pay attention.

• • •

How can you tell when the bride at a Jewish wedding is really ugly?

Everyone lines up to kiss the caterer.

• • •

What do you call a black woman who's had three abortions?

A crime buster.

• • •

What do you call a woman who's lost most of her intelligence?

Divorced.

• • •

How many feminists does it take to change a lightbulb?

Fourteen. Six to form a Women's Lightbulb Changing Committee, and eight to protest that changing lightbulbs is exploitation of women.

• • •

What do you call a gay lumberjack?

Spruce.

• • •

Why do blondes smile when they see lightning?

They think they're getting their picture taken.

• • •

Now That's Sick!

So a rabbi and a priest are walking down the beach in Miami. Suddenly, a sea lion walks past them, followed by a naked woman. Then, ten mice stroll into a restricted country club, followed by two Italians carrying pizzas.

Seeing this, the priest turns to the rabbi and opens his mouth to speak.

"Forget it, Father," the rabbi says. "I've already heard this one."

• • •

Why don't women have brains?

Because they don't have dicks to put them in.

• • •

Why do men cut holes in their pants pockets?

So they can run their fingers through their hair.

• • •

How do you know when a black woman reaches orgasm?

The next guy in line taps you on the shoulder.

• • •

What do you call a blonde with no arms, no legs, and no torso?

Muffy.

• • •

What's the definition of a really great nurse?

A woman who makes the patient without disturbing the bed.

• • •

Why is sodomy so easy?

Any asshole can do it.

• • •

What's the definition of a perfect marriage?

Your housekeeper and your wife both come a couple of times a week.

• • •

Why don't blondes eat bananas?

They can't find the zippers.

• • •

What's the best way to train your girlfriend to give oral sex?

Tie her hands behind her back and make her eat spaghetti.

Now That's Sick!

Why do fags love hamburgers?

Because it's hot meat between two nice buns.

• • •

A five-year-old child crawls onto Santa's lap at the local Wal-Mart.

Santa asks the five-year-old, "And what do you want for Christmas, little girl?"

The kid replies, "I want a Barbie and a G.I. Joe."

"But little girl, Barbie doesn't come with G.I. Joe," Santa says.

"Yes, she does," the little girl insists.

"Barbie doesn't come with G.I. Joe, she comes with Ken," Santa tells her.

"No," the little girl says. "Barbie does come with G.I. Joe. She only fakes it with Ken."

• • •

So three mice are sitting in a bar.

The first mouse says, "I'm so tough, I stole the cheese from the mousetrap before the trap slammed down on my neck." He knocks back a shot of bourbon.

The second mouse says, "You know those little mouse tablets that kill us on sight? I'm so tough, I ate one of 'em whole!" He, too, knocks back a shot of bourbon.

The third mouse slips off his barstool and starts to walk out of the bar. The first mouse asks him, "Hey, where are you going?"

The third mouse replies, "I'm going home to fuck the cat."

Why are students frisked in the New York City public schools?

So they can give you a gun if you don't already have one.

● ● ●

How can you tell when a chick has been jerking off with a cucumber?

When the salad comes, so does she.

● ● ●

How do you know when you're really a loser?

On your wedding night, your bride says she wants to date other men.

● ● ●

How does a guy know when he's really in love?

He divorces his wife.

● ● ●

Why do women like men who've pierced their ears?

They've experienced pain and bought jewelry.

● ● ●

So the third grader comes running home from school. He bursts into the family trailer home and says to his mother, "Mama, we all went swimming today."

Mama says, "That's nice, Billy Bob."

"And you know what, Mama? I got me the biggest pecker in the whole third-grade class."

"I ain't surprised, son," his mother remarks.

"Why's that, Mama?"

"I reckon," his mother says, "it's cause you're seventeen."

• • •

So then there's this guy whose penis is too long— his girlfriend can't handle it. As it turns out, he also has a terrible stuttering problem.

He goes to see his doctor, who says, "Your stutter is caused by the fact that your dick is too long. If I cut four inches off it, both of your problems will be solved."

The guy tells his doctor, "Let's give it a try."

A week later, the guy comes back and says, "Doc, it only half worked. My stutter is gone, but my girl-friend says my dick isn't big enough to satisfy her. Maybe you'd better give me back those four inches."

The doctor says, "F-F-Fuck you."

• • •

How do you know when you're at a high-class wedding in Tennessee?

The bride's veil covers most of her overalls.

• • •

How many rednecks does it take to screw in a lightbulb?

What's a lightbulb?

• • •

What's the difference between a lawyer and a prostitute?

A prostitute stops fucking you when you're dead.

• • •

Do you know how to save a lawyer from drowning?

If you don't, good!

• • •

What's the difference between a Harley and a Hoover vacuum cleaner?

The position of the dirt bag.

• • •

What do you get when you cross a lesbian and a lawyer?

An attorney who won't fuck you.

Now That's Sick!

So a rabbi, a priest, and a lawyer are on a sinking ship. As they try to find a lifeboat, the rabbi says, "Children first!"

The lawyer says, "Fuck the children!"

The priest says, "Do you think we have time?"

• • •

So a housewife, an accountant, and a lawyer are asked how much two plus two equals.

The housewife says, "Four."

The accountant says, "I'm not sure. Let me run those figures through my spreadsheet one more time."

The lawyer lowers his voice and says, "How much do you want it to be?"

• • •

Why do women fake orgasms?

Because they think we care.

• • •

What do you call a lawyer with an IQ of 50?

Your Honor.

• • •

So your mother-in-law and your lawyer are trapped in a burning building, and you have time to save only one of them. What do you do?

Go catch a movie.

How do you know a Deadhead's been to your house?

He's still there.

• • •

Hear about the flasher who was thinking about retiring?

He decided to stick it out a little longer.

• • •

So God is trying to decide where to go on vacation. He remarks to one of His angels, "I just don't know where to go. I've been everywhere."

The angel says, "I hear Alpha Centauri's nice this time of year."

God says, "I've been there."

"How about Mars?" the angel says.

"I went there last year," God replies.

"How about Earth?" the angel inquires.

"Nah," God says. "The last time I was there, I knocked up this Jewish chick and they're still talking about it."

• • •

What has four balls and eats ants?

Two uncles.

• • •

Now That's Sick!

How do you get a nun pregnant?

Dress her up like an altar boy.

• • •

What's the difference between meat and fish?

When you beat your fish, it dies.

• • •

What comes after 69?

Listerine.